ACADEMY OF
LEARNING

Your Complete Preschool Lesson Plan Resource: Volume 7

© 2015 Breely, Crush & Associates, LLC

Ver. 112214

Table of Contents

Educator Biography

Sharlit Elliott has a B.S. in Elementary Education and Early Childhood from Brigham Young University and has been a teacher for over 15 years working with children ages 3-5. She keeps current on changes in education by attending University classes and conferences several times a year. Besides having raised five children, she has held various leadership positions with the Girl Scouts and the 4-H program. She enjoys gardening, scrapbooking, reading and of course working with children.

How to Use This Book

This book is designed for a teacher working with children ages 3-5 in a classroom, homeschool or home preschool environment. One of the most important aspects of this series is that it includes fun activities that will enhance their skills. These lessons plans, games and ideas are all for you to use. Don't forget, these are complete lessons and activities that have been designed for compliance with federal and state guidelines for education. We go above and beyond to bring you MORE than what's expected in the public school system.

We will refer to your students as "your children or class". That includes whatever area you are using these lessons for: homeschool or preschool. Our lesson plans include improving student's abilities through activities. The skills we will be working with include: listening skills, music, movement, language and literacy, mathematics, science, fine motor, creative art, sensory, dramatic play, and social skills.

The book is organized by themes which will help you quickly find just the right information. The headings in the book will direct you quickly to large group, small group, and free time activities. It will also provide ideas for field trips.

This book will include the following areas:

Group Activities/Circle Time

- Music & Movement is used to help develop large muscles in arms and legs. These need to be developed before children can be successful in small muscles activities such as used in writing or cutting with scissors. This area also helps children learn to enjoy music and the basics such as beat, loud/soft and fast/slow.

- Language & Literacy is how we help children learn vocabulary, story order, thinking skills, recall, concepts of the theme, and expressive language.

Small Group Activities/Table Times

- Math & Cognitive is used to teach numbers, shapes, patterns, sorting, thinking and reasoning skills.

- Fine Motor Skills develop small muscles to be able to draw, write, manipulate small things, to tear, and to cut with scissors.

- Language & Literacy is used to develop skills such as expressive writing, visual memory, matching letters, letter sounds, categorizing items, directional words, and opposites.

- Other creative activities to develop their own uniqueness as an individual.

Free Time

- Creative arts to draw, build, and develop their imagination.

- Sensory activities are used to learn through exploration and using their senses.

- Dramatic Play & Social Development let children take on different roles, solve problems, find solutions, and develop social interactions.

- Science helps children explore by experimenting, identifying problems, guessing what will happen, checking to see what did happen, questioning how things happened, and developing a plan of what to do next.

- Gross Motor Skills to practice using large and small muscles in fun activities.

- Field Trip Ideas to help children use real places to learn about the world.

Throughout the book we will use the following icons to show the different types of activities:

MUSIC & MOVEMENT

LANGUAGE & LITERACY

MATH & COGNITIVE

FINE MOTOR SKILLS

CREATIVE ARTS

SENSORY

DRAMATIC PLAY & SOCIAL DEVELOPMENT

SCIENCE

GROSS MOTOR SKILLS

FIELD TRIP IDEAS

                               www.academyoflearningonline.com

Forest Animals

GROUP ACTIVITIES/CIRCLE TIME

🎵 MUSIC AND MOVEMENT

"Oh, I Wish I Were" from Macmillian Sing & Learn Program by Newbridge Communications, Inc. Make animal headbands for the children to wear while they do the animal actions on the tape.

"Bluebird, Bluebird" from Songs that Teach by Beth Black, Susan H. Kenny, Patricia H. Nielsen, Rosalie R. Pratt. Eden Hill Publishing. Page 10.

This is a Texas Folk song where children stand in a circle holding hands while singing "Blue-bird, blue-bird, go through my win-dow. This is repeated three times. Then they sing "and buy molasses can-dy."

Next the children sing "Take a little (girl/boy) and tap (her/him) on the shoulder three times. The children or child tapped becomes the bluebird and goes around the circle trying to get inside the circle.

The children in the circle hold each others hand while raising and lowering their arms to open and close the window. When their arms are up the windows are open, so the bluebirds can fly into the circle under their raised arms. The children are singing "Take a little girl/boy and tap her/him on the shoulder" three times.

Then the children sing "and buy molasses candy." Now continue by singing the song again and doing the actions, so that all the children have a turn being the bluebirds.

"The Frog Song" from Macmillan Sing & Learn Program by Newbridge Communications, Inc. Children enjoy this song and jump like frogs.

"Rabbit Dance" from Macmillan Sing & Learn Program by Newbridge Communications, Inc. This is another action song with movements like hopping, wiggling their noses and twitching their tails.

"Camouflage" from Macmillan Sing & Learn Program by Newbridge Communications, Inc. This song teaches that animals can hide from others by blending into the areas around them because of their coloring.

"Animal Homes" from Macmillan Sing & Learn Program by Newbridge Communications, Inc. This song has children becoming different animals and telling them to pretend to the described home for different animals.

"One Little Owl" from Macmillan Sing & Learn Program by Newbridge Communications, Inc. This is a fun counting song about owls.

"The Squirrel" from Macmillan Sing & Learn Program by Newbridge Communications, Inc. Prepare a picture of a squirrel for each child to use from a book or clipart. Explain that they will listen to the song and move their squirrel to the directions in the song. Example: make the squirrel go up the tree.

"Nutty Squirrel" from Macmillan Sing & Learn Program by Newbridge Communications, Inc. Hide paper peanuts or real peanuts around the room before singing this song. Tell the children to be the squirrels in this song and gatherer the hidden nuts, but don't eat them. When they each have found a few nuts have them come back to the rug. You can have them each count their nuts and help them write the number on a piece of paper by them. Then they can see who has more or less than they do and they can crack and eat them. Make sure no one is allergic to nuts before doing this activity. If anyone is allergic use plastic nuts to hide and something else to eat.

"The Cool Bear Hunt" from the CD *Dr. Jean Sings Silly Songs* by Dr. Jean. Children love to act out this fun song.

"Over In The Meadow" from the CD *Dr. Jean Sings Silly Songs* by Dr. Jean. Use animal pictures with this song.

"The Three Boppin' Bears Rap" from the CD *Dr. Jean Sings Silly Songs* by Dr. Jean.

"The Beaver Call" from the CD *Dr. Jean Sings Silly Song* by Dr. Jean.

"The Bear Went Over The Mountain" from the CD *Dr. Jean Sings Silly Song* by Dr. Jean.

"Rattlesnake" from CD *Tony Chestnut & Fun Time Action Songs*.

"Furry Squirrel" from CD *Touched by a Song* by Miss Jackie Music Company.

LANGUAGE AND LITERACY

White Owl, Barn Owl by Nicola Davies, Candlewick Press.

The Raggedy Red Squirrel by Hope Ryden, Lodestar Books.

The Deer in the Wood by Laura Ingalls Wilder, HarperCollins Publishers.

Raccoons for Kids by Jeff Fair, Gareth Stevens Publishers.

Raccoons and Ripe Corn by Jim Arnosky, A Mulberry Paperback Book.

Barn Owls by Patricia Whitehouse, Heinemann Library.

Busy, Busy Squirrels by Colleen Stanley Rose, Cobblehill Books/Duton.

Squirrels and Chipmunks by Allan Fowler, Children's Press.

It's a Baby Raccoon! by Kelly Doudna, ABDO Publishing Company.

White Rabbit's Color Book by Alan Baker, Scholastic Inc. A good book to use and review color mixing.

The Kissing Hand by Audrey Penn, Scholastic Inc. The story of mother raccoon helping her child to not be afraid of leaving her and going to school.

A Pocket Full of Kisses by Audrey Penn, Scholastic Inc. This book is the second book that continues from The Kissing Hand. These books are available on C.D. from Scholastic.

Possum's Harvest Moon by Anne Hunter, Scholastic Inc. This is a fun story that teaches children about a possum.

Just One! by Sam McBratney, Scholastic Inc. This is a good story using forest animals to teach about sharing.

Sassafras by Audrey Penn, Scholastic Inc.

Owl Babies by Martin Waddell, Scholastic Inc. This book teaches that owls hunt for food at night and feed their babies.

Animal Babies: A Counting Book by Daniel Moreton, Scholastic Inc. This book has great pictures that the children can count with you.

Whose Forest Is It? by Rozanne Lanczak Williams, Creative Teaching Press.

All About Deer by Jim Arnosky, Scholastic Inc.

I Wonder Why Skunks Are So Smelly and other neat facts about mammals by Deborah De Ford, Graymont Enterprises, Inc.

Blueberries For Sal by Robert McCloskey, Scholastic Inc.

As always, read the books you select before time and choose the ones that best meet the needs of the children. For example, if they need to review their counting skills choose a book like Animal Babies: A Counting Book. You could also focus on sharing and read the book Just One!

Another area children usually need help is learning how to get along with others. Often if someone is different from them, they may judge them as not as good as they are. The book Sassafras is a good book to show that we are different in some ways, but we are also the same in important ways. We can value the differences.

Another way to plan what to include in the theme would be to introduce the topic by asking questions to find out what the children know about forest animals. You could ask questions such as, "Children, can you tell me what a forest is? Who lives in a forest?" Then show pictures and talk about who lives there. You can then find out from the children which animals that they would like to learn about. Use books from the list provided or go to the library and find books that are about the animals that the children would like to learn about.

SMALL GROUP ACTIVITIES/TABLE TIMES

MATH & COGNITIVE

Order Animal Sizes

Obtain a picture of a forest animal from online or coloring book and enlarge it into four sizes. Use these pictures with the children by having them put them in order from smallest to largest.

Match the number

You will need forest animal pictures for this project. If you want the game to be harder, have all the same animal picture for each card set or use different animals for the match up pictures. Punch out forest animals on a die cut machine or make copies of animals. You will need to make sets for numbers 1-10 or 1-20.

Next, write numbers on the back of half of the pictures with a special pen that will not bleed through from the other side. (These types of pens are available in the scrapbook section of craft stores. One example of this type of pen is a Zig pen by Memory System.) On the other half of the picture cards, you will place small stickers to represent the numeral to match. Continue by adding correct numbers of stickers to the rest of the animal cards.

First use sets that the children are familiar with and add more numbers when the children are ready for larger sets.

Children will play the game by taking turns turning over two cards to make a match of the numeral with the correct number of stickers. It is played like a memory match game. Children will count the stickers and the teacher with the help of the children will determine if the sets match.

Name That Number

Teacher will use a half sheet of a poster board to make three sided doors in the poster at random places. The number of doors will depend on the abilities of the children in your class. They work well for numbers 1-10 and 1-20. Now draw a simple forest animal picture on the outside of each door, or use an animal sticker on each door.

Next, glue the door side with the blank side of the doors to the blank board around the outside edges. Then use a colorful pen to write a number behind each of the three sided doors. Do not write the numbers in order.

Now the fun begins! Children will take turns opening an animal door and naming the number behind the door. If the child does not know the number let the children help name the number. The child will continue opening doors until all of them have been opened and named. Then the next child that has been watching will have a turn. I usually have the children that can do most of the numbers at first, so the children that are next have had a little review before they have their turn. If you want, you can each of the children that participated an animal sticker or an animal fruit snack.

Measure That Animal

Teacher will prepare several large pictures of forest animals that are different sizes. Children will use a ruler to measure each animal. The teacher will show them how to use the ruler to measure. The teacher will also decide and tell them how to measure the animal. It may be measured from side to side or from top to bottom.

After each measurement, the teacher will help the child write the number that represents the size of the picture on a sticky note. Then the child will place the sticky note on the picture that they measured. After all of the pictures have been measured have the child with your help arrange the pictures in order size according to the numbers written on the sticky notes. Talk about biggest and smallest sizes.

Count the Animals

The teacher will buy small plastic animals from a school supply store, dollar store or if they cannot find any, use a bag of colored circle shaped cereal. Place the animals or a bowl of the cereal in front of the child and show them how to put the animals or cereal in a line so that they can count them. They can sort the animals or the colored cereal into groups first or into a long line. Make sure that the task isn't too big for them to accomplish by limiting their amount of animals or cereal. Help them when needed to count, but be sure to have them say the number after you say the number.

FINE MOTOR SKILLS

Animal Foot Prints

Teacher will obtain wood blocks, foam sheets and rubber cement at a craft store to make stamp pads. Use a book on animal footprints to see how to make different animal footprints of forest animals. You can see my example on my wood blocks below. Use a copy machine to enlarge the footprints for you to copy. Then place the paper pattern on top of a doubled layer of foam and cut the foam using the paper as a pattern. Glue the doubled foam footprints first to each other and then on to the center of the wood block. You now have a stamp of an animal footprint. Do this same procedure with the other foot print patterns. I made a deer, fox, squirrel, and rabbit footprint. They are not similar to each other so it's easier for the children to identify.

You make the ink pad by taking a paper towel and folding in half and then in half again. Then place it on a small foam plate. Now, mix a color of poster paint with a small amount of dish soap. Place the paint on top of the folded paper towel and work it into the towel. Now the children can press the animal stamp block onto a piece of paper and print the animal's footprint.

Children can do this as a group project onto a long piece of butcher paper to show the different animals and where they walked or as an individual project on a large piece of water color paper.

Talk with the children before they make prints and show the blocks with the prints on them and show pictures of the animals represented. Have them look carefully at the animal's feet and see if they can match up the block print with correct animal. If they can't match them, show the pictures again and point out the various characteristics of each animal. Then show them the correct block and point out those characteristics.

Animal Puppet

Provide lunch sacks, pens or markers, colored construction paper, scissors, glue, pieces of different types of material such as fake fur, fleece, buttons or eyes. This is a big project, so it can be completed over a few days.

Children will create an animal head from the construction paper. They can draw a circle head or body parts such as arms, a tail, or ears. Then they can glue the parts onto the lunch sack. So they will not create the puppet upside down, help children be aware that their hand will fit in the sack and will form the body part.

Next they can cut from different materials and glue onto them onto their puppet. When they are finished have them clean up their area and place their completed puppet in a safe place to dry. Later, when the puppets have dried, have the children take turns showing their animal puppets to other children in the circle.

Have them tell the name of their animal and what their animal eats or something else about their animal. Write what they say about their animal on a sheet of paper that they can take home with their animal puppet. If there is time when they have completed them, you can invite their families to the class. They can be there when the children show them at circle and talk about them.

Forest Texture Picture

Teacher will use small glue bottles to mix different food colors or use liquid water colors in the bottles. Mix a variety of colors that you would find in a forest. Teacher will also cut square and/or rectangle shapes from cardboard boxes. These shapes can be left plain for them to use or can be covered with colored butcher paper.

The children will use the small glue bottles to create their own forest of trees, animals, and/or plants onto the square or rectangle boards. Make sure that they are left flat to dry so that the glue will not run. Hang them up in your room when they are dry.

Forest Diorama

The teacher will collect shoe boxes for each of the children to use. Ask parents to bring one or more shoe boxes if they have them or check at places that sell shoes for any shoe boxes that they no longer need. Or you can purchase them at office supply or box supply stores. Prepare the boxes by cutting a hole in one end of the boxes. You can also ask parents to cut the holes in their child's box. The hole is where you look through to see the scene created.

This activity will take several days to complete. Explain to the children that they will be creating a forest inside their box and that they will look through their hole to see inside the box. You can purchase small animals for them to glue inside it or have them draw their own animals and have them cut them out and tape them inside the box. They can also glue sand to the bottom of their box for the soil.

Next they can draw trees and plants on paper you supply to cut and tape into box. Another choice of props could be made by children using different colors of chenille and small artificial flowers to cut and shape into trees and plants and then placed inside their forest.

When they are all completed have them on display for all to see and the children to tell about their own diorama.

LANGUAGE AND LITERACY

Questions and Answers

At circle time each day select a few pictures of common forest animals to show the children. Then ask the children the name of an animal. Ask other questions to determine what they already know about the animal shown, such as: What does this animal eat? Where might this animal sleep? Who knows what their babies might be called? When do they sleep?

Write down what they want to learn about this animal and place the child's name by their questions. During the day find that child and help them look with you through books to find the answers to their question. Go over the answer with them until they are confident in answering their question. Later during a circle time take turns with a few of the children one at time by reading one of their questions. Have that child come up to the front and tell others the answer he/she found to their question. If they found pictures too, have the child show them.

Continue doing this each day until all the children with questions have had a turn to tell others the information that they found.

Forest Memory Match

The teacher will make cards by using index cards that have forest two matching animal cards of six to ten cards. The pictures can use matching forest animal clip art, die cut animals, drawing, or animal stickers. Animal stickers can be found at school supply stores or from various stores online. They last longer if you laminate them or cover them with clear contact paper. Then they can also be cleaned with disinfectant wipes.

If the children are new at this game, use only four matching cards. Then, when they get better at making matches, use up to ten matches at a time. To begin, play place the cards face down in several lines on the table in front of a few children.

Children will play the game by taking turns, turning over two cards one at a time. They will say the name of the animals that they tried to match. If they did not make a match they will turn their cards back over. If they make a match they will take the two matching cards and put them in front of them on the table. Then they will try again. They will continue playing as before until they no longer make a match.

The next child will take their turn as before. Remind the children to try and remember where the cards were, so that they can match them when it's their turn. Also remind them to say the names of the animals when they turn the cards over. Play continues until all of the cards have been matched and named.

Name That Animal

The teacher will prepare some simple facts about some animals and things you might see in a forest. Then make about three statements for each of the animals and end with the question - "What am I?" some examples follow: I work to build dams in ponds and in rivers. I am busy. I have sharp teeth. What am I? (Beaver)

I store food for the winter when snow comes. I have a bushy long tail. I can hold nuts in my cheeks. What am I? (Squirrel)

I work very hard. I can carry a load bigger than I am. I have three body parts. What am I? (Ant)

I wash my face with my paws, but I don't eat with a spoon. I look like I'm wearing a mask, but I'm not. I hunt for my food at night. What am I? (Raccoon)

I am as busy as can be. My wings go so fast that they make a sound. I love to be in the flowers. What am I? (Bee)

I have spots when I'm a baby, but they go away when I'm grown. I like to eat in the meadow. I can run and jump very high. What am I? (Deer)

Place all your questions on individual cards. Place the cards on the floor near you face down. Have a small group of children sit in a circle with you. Tell the children that they will take turns choosing a card from the floor. The teacher will read the card to that child and have her/him

Guess what animal it is. If the child does not know the answer, have him or her ask you questions about the animal (such as, "how big is it?"). If the child does not get the answer after asking two questions, have the children in the circle raise their hands. Have the child then pick one of them to name the animal. If they need more help, tell them more information. Whoever guesses the animal gets to get up and act like the animal.

Encourage them to use movements and noises where possible. Play continues with a new child picking an animal card.

Preposition Actions

Children will be in a small group. The children will act out the actions. Teacher will say a child's name and then a direction for the child. Examples: Mary, walk <u>around</u> the other children. Mark, stand <u>between</u> Sam and John. Susan, lay on the floor. Cindy, sit <u>under</u> the table. Children, make a circle by joining hands and Mike go <u>in</u> the circle. Now Ellen go <u>out</u> of the circle. Rosa, hold your hand <u>over</u> Mateos head. Children, line up <u>behind</u> the chair. Now line up <u>in-front</u> of the chair.

Prepositions are hard for children to understand, so play this like a game often so that they can learn the meaning of these works.

Book Making

Supply the children with markers and paper. Ask them to draw a picture of something that we have talked about this week, like a forest, an animal, or a book that we read. Tell them that after they have finished their drawing to tell a teacher or helper about their picture, so that we can write their words down to make a class book. Tell them that you will collect all their pages together to make a class book. Also tell them that you will read the book to the class and mention the name of the person who did it.

After you collect all the pages put them in order into a binder. Read them first before reading it to the class, so that you are familiar with it. That way you will not stumble over their words. After reading the book, place it with your library books so the children can look at it and try to read it. They love the books that they make and enjoy hearing their words read.

FREE TIME

CREATIVE ARTS

Teacher will supply black and blue construction paper with colored chalk. Ask the children to choose to make a day or night time picture of whatever they would like. They can use the chalk as is or if they would like, supply small water containers, so that they can dip their chalk into the water. They will be able to see that the lines are different when they use water to dip their chalk.

Another activity would be to set up the easel with paper, water and watercolor sets. Encourage the children to draw whatever they would like. If they ask for help, show them how to press the watercolor brush against the side of the container so that it will not run as much. Also show them if they ask a few simple ways to make grass or trees. Be careful not to show them it should be a certain way. Make a few different ways that aren't fully developed. You don't want them to copy, but you do want them to have some idea of how to make any basic shape.

SENSORY

Depending on the time of year you may want sand in tubs or flour to represent snow. Add small plastic forest animals and trees. Small thin tree branches can become trees for the sensory table. You can also use small artificial plants for trees and scrubs. If you can find small people to add that would be great or add Fisher Price people. If you choose the flour for the snow a few of the days you could put a flour sifter for the children to create a snow storm. Children could also create caves for the animals using upside down berry basket with material over them or other materials. You could also have small stainless steel mirrors, so that the children could make ponds for the animals to drink. Tell the children come up with their own ideas to add to the tubs or sand table.

DRAMATIC PLAY & SOCIAL DEVELOPMENT

For this area it is fun to use a small tent. When you set it up be sure and make the rules clear for its use. If you don't have one you can use a card table with a sheet over it for a tent. Bring old pots and pans for pretend cooking on the campfire. Wood blocks can be use for the pretend fire. You can use red clear cellophane for the flames. Children like to dress up to play here. Red plaid flannel shirts or hunting type shifts can be found at thrift shops, as well as caps for the pretend campers. Plastic food can also be used for camping with plates, cups and spoons. Also provide flash lights, old cameras, and binoculars. The pretend area can also include stuffed forest animals and/or puppets to interact.

You may have to use a timer and limit the number of children at this area because it is such a fun place to be. Let the children know that they can have a turn because you will keep this special area up all week or longer if they are still enjoying it. Have the children write their name on a list and cross off their name after they have a turn playing there. This area encourages imagination, creativity, and language skills.

SCIENCE

This is a good time to talk about different types of rocks. The teacher will supply junior non-fiction books and put them on display. Your local library usually has many good books to check out. Teacher will also gather rocks and the children will also collect and bring rocks to the classroom. If any of the parents have a rock collection, encourage them to bring it and share simple things about them with the children. This would be great way for the children to learn and explore.

You can buy nice rock posters at the school supply stores. Then the children can use the poster to match up rocks to the pictures of different rocks. The posters should have labeled pictures of rocks, so that the children can label some of rocks. Also have a shallow bowl of water for the children. The children can use it for dipping their rocks so they can see how they look when they are wet. The children could also use a balance scale to see which rocks are heavier than the other rocks. They can also learn how many of the lighter rocks it would take to have the scale even in balance. Scales also can be bought at school supply stores.

GROSS MOTOR SKILLS

The teacher will use nuts in shells for this activity. If any child is allergic to nuts use plastic fake nuts. The teacher will prepare by hiding the nuts ahead of time either in their room or outside in a confined area. The teacher will also make headbands for each child with construction paper and attach small triangle ears to the headband. He/she will also obtain a box for a pretend tree and cut a hole in it for a nest. If time allows, paint the tree brown with poster paint or if you have a volunteer have him/her do it for you.

When all is ready, talk about how squirrels prepare for the winter by collecting nuts and putting them in a special place to store them for the winter. Tell children that they are going to pretend to be squirrels and find nuts to store for the winter. Give them each a headband to wear. Then show them the hollow tree trunk and explain that they will place their nuts in there. Tell them that when you call them, "Squirrels, squirrels come on home." They will all come to the tree. Then they will get all the nuts out and count them.

Next two of three children that you pick with hide all the nuts again while the rest hide their eyes by folding their arms and putting their head onto their arms. Tell the children that are hiding them, to place them in the same confined area as before. They should also come back to the tree as soon as their nuts have been hidden. The children that hid the nuts stay at the tree while the rest of the children find the nuts and put them in the tree hole.

Stop the game before they tire of it and play it again another day. Next time you play the game, you can play it the same way or you can use varies actions to play the game such as hoping on one or two feet like a rabbit, skipping, running like a deer, or crawling like a snake to find their food. The food can vary.

FIELD TRIP IDEAS

Check out areas that may have wood or forest animal near by such as parks, fields and back yards if you live in an area in the foothills. If you can't locate any, ask parents if they know of places near by. You can go to parks that have trees and flowers. Have the children sit quietly and listen to the birds and observe them and see bees and butterflies.

Take blankets for the children to sit on to rest and have a snack on. Prepare a snack to take with you that forest animals would like too, such as nuts, sunflower seeds, berries and carrots. Talk about what different animals would like your snack. Also provide cool water and small paper cups for them. Be sure and take a garbage bag and explain the importance of keep the earth clean for people and animals.

Bears/Science

GROUP ACTIVITIES/CIRCLE TIME

MUSIC AND MOVEMENT

"Bear Went Over The Mountain" from *Dr. Jean Sings Silly Songs* CD.

"The Cool Bear Hunt" from *Dr. Jean Sings Silly Songs* CD. Children love this new version of "The Bear Hunt" after they learn the older one. The actions to this song are fun and easy to follow without having to learn the words.

"The Three Boppin' Fear Rap" from CD Dr. Jean Sings Silly Songs.

"Yogi Bear" from CD *Just For Fun!* by Dr. Jean.

"The Bear Hunt" from The Learning Station CD *Here We Go Loopty Loo*.

"Brown Bear, Brown Bear, What Do You See?" by Bill Martin Jr., CD in Book Special Combination. This song helps children review color names. Hold up the book and sing the words in the book with or without the CD. The pages show different colored animals on each page and the song repeats the color of the animal before going on to the next page. You can make your own cards to use with the songs by coping pictures of animals and coloring them the colors mentioned in the song.

"Boris the Singing Bear" from CD *Touched by a Song* by Miss Jackie Music Company.

"A Favorite Thing" from Macmillan Sing & Learn Program by Newbridge Communications, Inc. This is a fun song sleeping with a teddy bear. Have the children hold hands and form a circle. Then have them drop hands and provide them with a stuffed animal like a teddy bear to hold and sway with while listening to the song. You can also have the children bring their own stuffed animal to class this day to use with the song.

You can have fun teaching children to make up their own songs to traditional songs such as "One, Two, Buckle My Shoe" and "Ten Little Indians." Here is a song you can sing with the children to the tune of "Diddle Diddle Dumpling My Son John":

Diddle diddle dumpling, my little bears

Diddle diddle dumpling, my little bear,

Went to bed with his hat on.

One eye closed and a bat in his hand,

Diddle diddle dumpling, my little bear.

"Counting To Ten" from Macmillan Sing & Learn Program by Newbridge Communications, Inc. This song will have the children taking giant steps, giant jumps and giant hops. They will move while counting with the beat of the song.

"Walking to the ABC's" from Macmillan Sing & Learn Program by Newbridge Communications, Inc. This song invites children to practice their ABC's by walking, stomping and tip-toeing to the beat. The tune's beat and activity helps them not run the letters together while singing them.

"Color Hoedown" from Macmillan Sing & Learn Program by Newbridge Communications, Inc. This song gets the children moving and learning the colors red, yellow and blue. The teacher will make bear necklaces for each child by using pattern in the Macmillan Sing & Learn Program by Newbridge Communications, Inc. or you can make a simple circle for the head with small circle ears, eyes, nose, and mouth. Then copy the bear head onto colored paper and cut them out, laminate them and put yarn through a hole punch for the children to wear. Then show them the action that each color does in the song. Give each of the children a colored necklace to wear. Practice the actions before playing the song. Help them listen to the song to learn when the colors will be sung. Now play the song and have fun!

LANGUAGE AND LITERACY

<u>Brown Bear, Brown Bear, What Do You See?</u> by Bill Martin Jr./Eric Carle, Henry Holt and Company 1995. This is a wonderful book to learn rhyming, colors and animal names.

<u>Black Bear Cub</u> by Alan Lind, Smithsonian Wild Heritage Collection. Scholastic Inc. 1997.

<u>You and Me, Little Bear</u> by Martin Waddell, Scholastic Inc. 1996.

<u>Let's Go Home Little Bear</u> by Martin Waddell, Scholastic Inc. 1991.

<u>Can't You Sleep Little Bear?</u> by Martin Waddell, Scholastic Inc. 1988.

<u>Thank You, Brother Bear</u> by Hans Baumann, Scholastic Inc. 1995.

<u>The Bear Went Over the Mountain</u> adapted by Rozanne Lanczak Williams, Creative Teaching Press, 1994.

<u>Blueberries For Sal</u> by Robert McCloskey, Caldecott Honor Book. Scholastic Inc. 1987.

<u>The Berenstain Bears Forget Their Manners</u> by Stan & Jan Berenstain. Random House 1985. This book and the others following help preschool children learn various topics listed in their title. My children really enjoyed listening to them. Pick this up at garage sales or on line.

<u>The Berenstain Bears Get In A Fight</u> by Stan & Jan Berenstain. Random House 1983.

<u>The Berenstain Bears Meet Santa Bear</u> by Stan & Jan Berenstain. Random House. 1984.

<u>The Berenstain Bears' New Baby</u> by Stan & Jan Berenstain. Random House. 1974.

<u>The Berenstain Bears Learn About Strangers</u> by Stan & Jan Berenstain. Random

House. 1985.

The Berenstain Bears and Too Much Junk Food by Stan & Jan Berenstain. Random House. 1985.

The Berenstain Bears Count Their Blessings by Stan & Jan Berenstain. Random House. 1995.

Corduroy by Don Freeman. Scholastic Inc. 1989.

A Pocket For Corduroy by Don Freeman. Scholastic Inc. The two books about Corduroy teach about kindness and show that different people have the same feelings.

The Bear Went Over the Mountain and other Bear Songs by Read With Me Paperbacks. Scholastic Inc. 1995. This book has finger plays, movements, stories, and songs. It also comes with a tape.

The Teddy Bears' Picnic Song arranged and performed by Jerry Garcia & David Grisman, Illustrated by Bruce Whatley. This book tape is by Harper Collins Publisher. 1996.

The Mitten adapted and illustrated by Jan Brett. Scholastic Inc. This book also can include a tape. 1990.

The Three Bears. You will find this book adapted by many illustrators at your own library. The children love this book. Just find your favorite online or at your library.

The Little Mouse, The Red Ripe Strawberry, and THE BIG HUNGRY BEAR by Don and Audrey Wood. Scholastic Inc. 1994.

SMALL GROUP ACTIVITIES/TABLE TIMES

MATH & COGNITIVE

Crystal Garden

Teacher supplies: charcoals or sponges cut into 3 by 3 inches, shallow bowl (old ones you have or ones from thrift store), salt, bluing (found in laundry soap part of grocery store), ammonia (also found in cleaning section of store), food coloring (optional), and water.

Day #1 – Do this for each container you want to have. Place sponge or charcoal in a shallow bowl. Then pour sponge or coals 2 TB each of bluing, salt, water and ammonia. Caution children not to touch or move container around materials could hurt them if got into their eyes. I would keep it up high when an adult won't be there to watch it. Label this bowl #1. Have children draw a picture of how it looks and ask them what they think might happen.

Now use another dish and place charcoals or sponge (the same one you used in dish #1) and pour 2 TB of salt, bluing, water, but not ammonia. Label this #2. Have the children draw and label how this looks and ask what they think might happen.

Next, use a dish and proceed with the sponge or coal (the same one as used before) and leave out the bluing (but do add the ammonia). Label this dish #3. Have the children make drawings and predictions as before. Continue on by doing same as before for #4, but add all ingredients except the salt. Have the children make drawings with labels and ask questions.

Day#2 – Add 2 TB salt to container 1, 2, and 3, but not 4. Have them draw each dish again and note any changes. Ask them what they see and how they are different. Ask them what will happen next.

Day #3 – Add 2 TB each of bluing, salt, water and ammonia to dish #1. To dish #2 add all ingredients except the ammonia. To dish #3 add all ingredients except bluing. To dish #4 add all ingredients except salt. Have the children continue to make drawings of the changes. Ask them what they think is happening in each dish and why. This day you can also if you like have them add a drop of food coloring to each dish.

Day #4 – Point out that all the dishes except #1 did not grow. Ask them what might happen if we added all the ingredients to each dish what might happen. Will they grow? How much if any and why or why not? Proceed by adding all the ingredients and watching them one more day.

Day #5 – Have them look at all their drawings and compare what happened. Have them tell you their conclusions. Tell them that they are scientist now.

Science Experiment With Raisins

Supplies: seedless green grapes, raisins, foil, balloons, masking tape, small zip lock bags, small bowl with water.

Show the children the raisins and ask if them what they know about them. Tell them that they will be experimenting to see if we can make raisins. Have the children place a few raisins on the foil and place them on a sunny spot by a window. Tell them that they need to check them each day to see if there are any changes. If there is not enough heat from the sun use a lamp with a light close to them for heat.

When the grapes have dried up to make raisins, have the children taste them, but save a few to use later. Then review the steps using a balloon. In advance, prepare the balloon by filling it with water and tie the end closed. Now cover the balloon with clear wide tape. Place a dish pail and large needle nearby.

Call the children over and tell them that the balloon represents a grape. Tell them that the heat from the sun or light made the juice dry up inside the grape. Have children take turns pushing the needle into the pretend grape. Now have them take turns squeezing the grape over the dishpan. As the balloon (grape) grows smaller, have them observe the many wrinkles. Show the left over grapes that they dried and have them compare the pretend one to theirs. Ask them to explain how they made the grapes.

Learn How To Make Colors

Use the book White Rabbit's Color Book by Alan Baker. Teacher assembles three zip lock bags for each child, a can of shaving cream, and food colors red, yellow, and blue. Read the first two pages of the book. Now give each child a bag with a small amount of saving cream and a drop of the yellow food coloring. Teacher will close it tightly and caution the children to carefully mix it by squeezing. Ask the children what color they made.

Now read the next two pages and give each child a drop of red into their yellow bag. Ask them if the color will change and if so what the new color will be. Now have the lid to bag closed tightly and carefully squeeze the mixture. Ask what happened.

Place red in a clean bag with shaving cream for each child and have them mix carefully as before. Show and read the page in the book of rabbit going in to the red bowl. Then turn the page that shows the rabbit going into the blue bowl. Turn page again and ask what color the rabbit will be. Now put blue into their bag with the red and have the mix as before. Show the next page with the purple rabbit. Ask did you make purple too and ask what colors made the new color.

Next turn the page again and give bags with shaving cream and blue food coloring in it. Then add yellow food coloring to their bags. Close as before and mix carefully. Ask what color they made and turn the page to show the green rabbit. Then open their now green bag and add red to their bag. Ask what color they will make now. Turn the page and ask what color their bag is and if it is the same color as the brown rabbit. If it's not the same color, ask why this may not be. Try adding more green or red to the bag to see if they can make it the same.

Review what they have learned by asking questions, and using their mixed bags and the book.

Dancing Pepper

Assemble these materials: balloons, plate with salt and pepper, string and wool clothing.

Teacher will blow up a balloon and tie it with the string. Then the children will take turns rubbing it onto the wool cloth. Now place the balloon near the prepared plate and have the children watch carefully to see if the salt and pepper move. Watch it over and over by rubbing with the wool again when needed. Ask them what is happening.

Rub another blown balloon with the wool or on their hair and place the balloon on the wall and see what happens. Tell the children that they made static electricity when they rubbed the balloon on the wool cloth and on their hair. The pepper and the salt were attracted and then repelled because of it.

Frost Can

Save a large can for this activity. Cover cutting edge with wide silver duct tape. Fill can to one or two inches from the top with water. Place it in the freezer over night. When you are ready to talk about frost set it on a table. Frost will form on the outside of it. Children can feel and see it. Talk about frost that forms on the grass in the winter. Talk about moisture in the can and in the ground and how it freezes to form the frost.

Learning About Air

Materials needed: balloon, fan, straw, feather, paper towel tube.

Ask children, "How do we know that there is air?" Then, turn on a fan and let the children feel it. Tell the children that you can feel its movement. Pass out straws or empty tubes and have children blow through them and place their hand over it to feel the air move.

Now place a feather in front of each child and have them blow on the feather and watch its movement. Ask the children if they have seen the wind blow the leaves outside.

Blow up a balloon and hold the end closed. Ask the children what will happen if you let go of the end. Then let go of the end. Ask why did the balloon move? Talk about how the wind going out of the balloon forces the air in front of it so the balloon could move.

Let them try to move different items in the classroom and report back to you what they could move and guess why they couldn't move heavy items. Talk about it and ask them to have several children blow at the same time to see if it made and difference. Tell the discussion going as long as there is interest.

Vinegar and Egg

Gently place a raw egg in a clear jar filled with white vinegar. Have the children watch what happens to the egg in the next four days. Each day have them touch the egg carefully for any changes.

In two days the shell should soften and begin to dissolve. By the fourth day the calcium should have completely dissolved, leaving only the bladder. Talk about vinegar being an acid and ask if they think it will dissolve other things.

Write down their suggestions of items to try to dissolve. Vote on the five most popular ones and try them out. Beside each bottle or glass have each of the children write their name and put yes or a no if they think it will or will not dissolve. Check the results and see what happens.

Number Game

Take a poster board and cut it into four equal parts. Use one section to make five or more columns going across and five or six columns going down. Write numerals from 1-10 (or whatever amount you would like the children to learn). Put circle punch colors across the top. There should be one color for each column or for the number of children that you would like to play the game at one time. See example.

Teacher will supply game markers (buttons or beans), dice or cut squares for each number. Write one number on each square or use the dice. Children shake the die and put marker next to that numeral in their assigned color column. If using number squares, place the squares upside down in a pile and have child draw the square on top and put their marker by that number in their color assigned column.

Play continues as each child takes a turn and draws or shakes dice putting a marker in their column. If they shake or draw a number that they already have you can have them just pass the die to the next player. Or you could have them shake or draw until they get a number that they don't have. It depends one how long you want the game to continue.

Play continues until one or two ways. One way would be until the first one has a marker on each of their numbers or when all the children have a marker on all of their columns. If it's taking too long for all of them to get the columns completed, let them take more turns. You can also take the number cards out that are not longer needed.

Using the die is the best way to have them play. They have to count the dots on the die and match that amount to the numeral on their column. You can use two dice for the game and have the columns longer to help them learn numerals 1-12. At the end of the year you can increase the number of die to reach 24 or more. You can also make columns starting with different amounts like 10-20. Have fun and variation by sometimes using other things for markers such as Cheerios and letting them eat some after the game.

FINE MOTOR SKILLS

Big Ripe Strawberry

After reading the book <u>The Little Mouse, The Red Ripe Strawberry, and THE BIG HUNGRY BEAR</u> by Don and Audrey Wood have the children draw a large strawberry. Then have strawberry-colored paint for them to color in the strawberry.

Jello paint can be made by adding *only* the hot water amount listed on a box of Jello to the Jello powder. Stir two minutes so it will be dissolved. Let it cool slightly in the fridge, so it won't be too runny. Then use paint brush or if you waited too long, use fingers. It smells just like a real strawberry and is shinny when dry.

Pocket For Corduroy Project

Teacher will read the book <u>A Pocket for Corduroy</u> before starting this activity. Teacher will make large pocket shapes on poster board and cut around them for tracers. Also set out colored construction paper. Glue, scissors, pencils, glitter or sequins, buttons and anything else you can think of that your children might like to use to decorate their pockets.

Children will trace around their pocket with a pencil on colored construction paper of their choice and then cut it out carefully. Now they will glue just around the edges and attach it to another piece of colored paper. Then they will decorate it using materials provided. They can also write their name on a piece of paper and slip it into their pocket. These pocket pictures look cute hung around the room. See example.

Mystery Writing

Teacher will provide white copy paper, white crayons, and watercolors with brush and small cups of water to rinse their brushes.

Children are instructed to write their names pressing hard with the white crayon of their paper. Then tell them the use whatever color of watercolor they would like to paint over their paper, but to make sure that their paint has a lot of water in it. It's fun for them to see their name pop out of the colored paint. Talk about how the wax in the crayon kept the watercolor from covering the wax in their written name. You can have them make designs and shapes again the paint over it or have them make designs and have them trade pictures with someone else, so they won't know what will appear. See example.

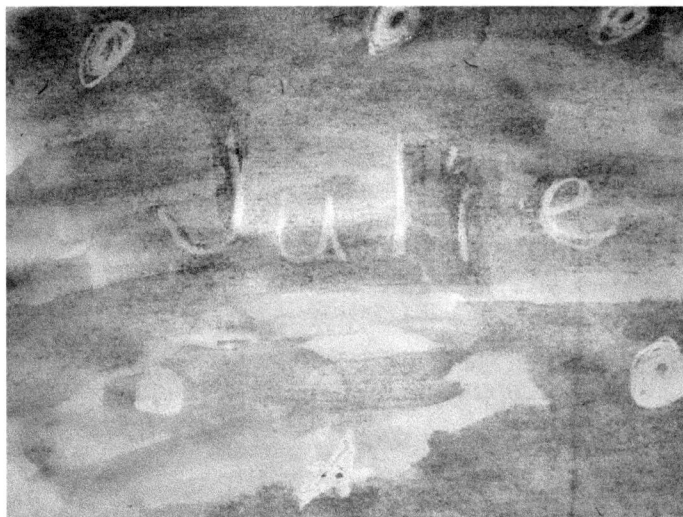

Magic Painting

Teacher preparation: long sheets of watercolor paper, poster paint in a variety of colors, plastic spoons to scoop and cups to mix paint with dish soap, magnetic balls, magnet wands, pencils, and large top lids from cardboard boxes. Line the inside of the box lids with wax paper.

Children will write their names on a piece of paper. They will then work with a partner to do this project. One child will place their paper with their name facing down inside the box lid. The other child will hold the lid and add four or five spoons full of paint and three or four magnetic balls to the inside of the box lid.

Now the other child, the one whose paper is in the box, will reach under the box lid and use the magic wand (magnetic wand) to move the balls through the paint and create a picture. Caution the child holding the box, to try and keep the box level, so the balls will stay in the box and not roll onto the floor. When that child has had a turn painting the two children will trade jobs and start the whole activity again.

Teddy Bear Picnic

Teacher will prepare for this activity by making a simple basket shape on a poster board. Then cut it out and trace around it to make a brown or another colored basket. Make one for each child. Have a parent help you prepare them if possible. Also find pictures of food in magazines or grocery aids. Put out scissors and glue.

Read to the children <u>The Teddy Bear Picnic</u>. Then, have children glue a cut out basket to a piece of colored construction paper carefully around the edges, so that they can put the pictures of the foods they want to take on their picnic in it. Set out the pictures on the pages and have them find and cut out the pictures of the foods that they want to take with them on their picnic. You can also have them just glue the basket to the paper and have them glue their cut pictures on the basket. See example.

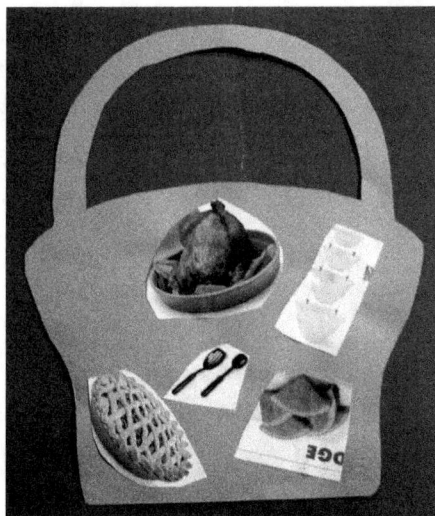

Bear Sewing

Draw a simple shape of the large bear or copy one from a coloring book or from clip art. Then make several copies of it. Cut out the bear shape leaving the line around the edge. Punch holes around the outline edges and laminate them. Now punch around again through the lamination. This makes it so it's not so hard to punch through the holes. Buy several long shoe laces for the children to use for sewing around the edges. You can also use yarn for sewing if you dip the ends in glue and dry them smoothed out or you can tape the ends of the yarn.

Have the children sew the bear on their own at first. Later show them how to go up and down with the yarn by turning it so that the yarn does not loop around the outside edge. Also show them how to sew without skipping holes and go continuously around the edge instead of skipping all over. Don't correct them too much at first so they don't get discouraged.

LANGUAGE AND LITERACY

Teddy Bear Picnic

After reading the book <u>The Teddy Bear's Picnic</u> children will plan a teddy bear picnic. Teacher will write down items on a large poster board. You can have the whole group at one time or better yet do this with a few children at a time in small groups. Use a new poster for each group so they don't just copy each others ideas. Help them think of ways they can prepare food in the class and things they could wear or bring, like a stuffed animal. Keep it simple like peanut butter sandwiches with milk and fruit for lunch and simple games like catch the ball or Duck, Duck, Goose. They could also wear pajamas or make and wear bear ears. Get them to plan what day to do it and where to do it. Lots of planning will be fun to get all involved. Be sure and ask or call on all the children in the class to participate. Children will tell you their ideas on food, games and what they could bring on this special day.

Later with the whole group read each poster and vote on the different ideas the children want to do or have. The winning items will be arranged for with their planning and help. Then just do it and have lots of fun!

Vocabulary Game

The teacher will prepare this game by cutting pictures from magazines on sporting good items, such as tents, Dutch ovens, fishing poles, bow & arrow, hiking boots, sleeping bags, camp stoves and etc. Mount them on card stock and laminate them for future use.

Now have a small group of children come to your table at one time. Show the pictures to the children one picture at a time. Have one child tell you what it is a picture of by raising their hand or go in around in a circle for children to answer. If you the children are raising their hands make sure that the same child is not always answering the questions. You want all of them to participate. Other questions to ask about the same picture would be: Tell me how it is used? Why is this important to have it with you? Tell what other things you could do with it and also different ways you could use. Talk about its qualities. Will it break? Is it hard or soft? How does it help you?

You can also use pictures of forest animals to do this game or any group of similar objects instead of pictures. One example would be items like cooking pan, small hatchet, work gloves, hiking boots, compass, camera, log and etc. Use questions as explained in picture ideas from above.

Making a Book

Teacher will cut out two matching large pictures of a bear outline on poster board. This will be the front and back of the class book. Then use that same pattern to cut pages for the children to use from watercolor paper. Punch two holes of the side so you can connect the pages together when the pages have been completed.

Have the children come to the table a few at a time. Tell them to draw something about a bear and tell you about their drawing. Tell them that you will be writing their words down on their sheet to put into a class book. Provide crayons for them to use. When they have finished drawing have them tell you about their picture.

Expand what they tell you by repeating the words in their sentence and having them to add to it. Example – Child says "Bear drink water." You say "The bear drinks water." Have the child tell where the water came from. Say "The bear drinks water from... The child says "River." You say, "The bear drinks water from the river." Continue on until child has given you three sentences. This activity will help children learn to express themselves.

When children's pages have all been completed, add them to the bear cover. Place them in order to make the collected writings into a story form. Add the back cover with all the pages connected with ring closure or yarn tied through them. Read the book to the class and then put it in your classroom library for the children to read.

Comprehension Story

Read the children a short story from a book that is only a few pages long and which has one line or less of print per page. Two examples of this type of book would be <u>The Three Friends And the Leaves</u> by Tomie dePaola, Scholastic, and <u>The Tree Friends And the Pumpkins</u> by Tomie dePaola, Scholastic.

Tell the children to listen closely to the story so that they will be able to answer three questions about the book. Then ask three simple questions such as the following: What were the colors that the leaves changed into? How many friends were in the story? What did the children do after playing in the leaves?

They can each answer one question about three different small books or answer all three questions from one book. After each small book's questions have been answered, read the book again. Have them see if they answered their question correct or if they can see a different answer to their question. Then proceed to the next book. You can also make up your own small book by adding words to a wordless picture book. You can find these types of books in your library. Your librarian will be able to help you.

Rhyming Words

Teacher will use a nursery rhyme book such as <u>Mother Goose</u>, Illustrated by Aurelius Battaglia, A Random House PICTUREBACK or <u>Three Little Kittens</u>, Illustrated by Lilian Obligado, A Random House PICTUREBACK. Read the book and select short rhymes such as "Hey Diddle, Diddle."

Teacher will read or say the riddle and the children will listen to hear which words sound alike. The teacher will clap if the word is the same as in diddle, diddle or if the words sound alike (diddle, fiddle). An example shown words that rhyme are underlined where to clap.

Hey diddle, <u>diddle</u>,

The cat and the <u>fiddle</u>,

The cow jumped over the <u>moon</u>,

The little dog laughed

To see such sport,

And the dish ran away with the <u>spoon</u>.

After reading and clapping, have the children listen to the rhyme again and have them clap with you. Then say just the words that rhyme together. Next have them listen to another rhyme and have them clap to the words that they think rhyme. Example below.

Pussy cat, <u>pussy cat</u>, where have you <u>been</u>?

I've been to London to look at the <u>queen</u>.

Pussy cat, <u>pussy cat</u>, what did you <u>there</u>?

I frightened a little mouse under her <u>chair</u>.

Now clap with them and ask them if they clapped where you did. Tell them they can listen to a few words that rhyme and then they will get a turn to rhyme some words.

Then you might say a word like rat, and then say rhyming words hat, bat, sat, cat. Now let them try some words that rhyme with pig. They might say wig, jig, big. It is okay if the say rhyming sounds that are not really words, such as tig, kig, mig. This will start a fun time for them as they think up and say many rhyming sounds and it will help them to hear rhyming words.

CREATIVE ARTS

Sponge Painting

Teacher will provide a pair of scissors and a small thin sponge for the each of the children to cut into different shapes. Also provide different colors of poster paint in small bowls. This paint should be mixed with a small amount of liquid dish soap. Provide aprons to protect the child's clothes. Show the child how to attach a clothes pin to their sponge design and help if needed.

Next have a colorful supply of paper for the children to choose from, to create their sponge prints on. They can overlap their sponge prints if they want. Also they can use the same color with the sponge or they can use other colors with their sponge. Be sure and have them place their names on the back. When they are dry they can display them around the classroom or take them home.

Glitter Pictures

Provide card stock paper for this process, small bottles of glue, and several different colors of glitter. Children will place their name on the back of their picture. Now children will create a glue design onto their paper. Then they will place their glue picture inside a large box lid with the glue side up. Then they will choose different colors of glitter to sprinkle onto their wet glue. When they are satisfied with their picture, they will carefully lift the picture up and let the extra glitter fall into the lid.

When the children have finished with the lids, the teacher will pour the remaining dry glitter into a bottle. This bottle will be a mixture of different colors and can be used again. You can save empty spice bottles to store glitter in and you can also use them as shakers for the glitter. Before children take these pictures home or mount them around the room make sure they are all the way dry. This may take several days, depending on how thickly the glue was applied.

Junk Art

The teacher will enlist the help of the parents in saving empty paper towel rolls, Styrofoam packing, empty egg cartons, plastic berry baskets, cardboard corners from packaging, and anything else you feel would good for the children to use.

Put out the items that you have collected. Also set out glue, tape, string, scissors, markers, and watercolor paints with small containers of water. Let the children make whatever they want. If they want to continue working on their project for more than one day, make a place for them to leave it there. It would be fun to take pictures of their completed project being sending them home. Then the pictures can be placed around the room for the children to see and remember.

SENSORY

Place sand in pails or the sensory table along with sand toy mold. Be sure and either wet the sand a little so that it will mold or place small water spray bottle with water for the children to wet the sand. Keep an eye on it to make sure that they don't spray too much water into it. If the children need help figuring out how to use the molds, show them how to pack the wet sand into the mold and carefully tip it over onto the flat sand surface. Gently tap the mold and it will fall out onto the sand. If it's too dry, add more water and if it's too wet wait for it to dry out a little in the sun.

You can use other things for molds like measuring cups, plastic cups, measuring spoons, small bowls, small Jello molds, plastic drinking glasses, and anything else that has an interesting shape that will hold sand.

DRAMATIC PLAY & SOCIAL DEVELOPMENT

Provide a small tent, cooking pans, pretend foods, teddy bears, dress up camping shirts, caps, table cloth, wood for pretend fire and anything else that you can collect to have a fun camping adventure such as cameras (old ones) and binoculars. If you don't have a small tent you can use a small table, such as a card table with an old blanket or sheet partially covering it. You want to be able to see the children at all times so make sure they know the rule of keep tent or covering open.

You may not have room for all the children to play in the area at the same time. Sharing can become too hard if it's over crowed, so make necklaces using yard with some type of punch out figure hanging from it such as a teddy bear. Then decide the maximum number that would be good for that area at one time and make that many necklaces for it.

Explain that they will be taking turns in the camping area and that they will need to have a special necklace on to play there. They can sign a paper with their name if they would like a turn. The teacher will set a timer to indicate when the children playing their need to stop, so that others can play. The teacher will help them put a line through their name when they have had a turn playing there. Teacher will also collect the necklaces they were using to give to the next children that signed the list. Keep the camping area up all week and longer if and of the children seem very interested, but take it down before it gets boring. Be sure and listening for sharing skill and vocabulary use, so that you can intervene when needed.

SCIENCE

Lava Jar

Teacher can demonstrate this first with a large jar and then have children make their own by using smaller jars. Use less of the ingredients for the smaller versions. Let children experiment by using less of the large jar ingredients to find out what works best for their size jar.

Before staring any experiment teach the children safety rules such as the following: Have an adult as your assistant, never taste an experiment unless an adult tells you that it is safe, keep your hands away from your mouth and eyes while working and wash them after wards.

Assemble these items for use: clear jar or jars, water source, food coloring, vegetable oil and salt shakers. Pour water until you reach the halfway mark. Add food coloring a few drops at a time until it is the shade you like. Now pour the oil into a measuring cup and then pour it a little at a time into the jar until it is about one inch thick.

Now watch carefully as you shake salt into the jar for about six shakes. The oil and salt will form a glob and sink to the bottom of the jar. As the salt dissolves in the water, the oil will float back to the top. Record how long it took so that next time you can use cold or hot water to see which works faster. Add more salt to watch the action repeat again.

This experiment works because water dissolves the salt and it can not dissolve the oil. The salt holds down the oil until it dissolves.

Bubble Fun

The night before make a bubble solution by mixing equal parts of liquid dish soap such as Dawn with water. Then add 1 to 2 tablespoons of sugar to the water-soap mixture.

The next day put some plastic wrap on the table in front of each child. Now use a plastic spray bottle to have children or you spray the wrap with plain water. Give each child a small container of the with bubble mix with a wand to dip into the mixture. Wands can be straws or PVC pipe.

Children will dip their wand into the solution and blow a half bubble onto their plastic wrap. Then they will blow bubbles inside of their bubbles. Children will see if the bubbles are all round or different shapes and if they can see other shapes inside their bubbles.

Leaf Color

Children will collect leaves in the fall. Then they will sort leaves into piles of the same colors. Teacher will have small baby food jars for the children to place each color of leaf individually in the jars. Have them fill the jars very full. Ask the children if they think that the colors will come out of the leaves if by putting water in them. Then fill the jars with water and glue the lids onto them. Check them each day.

Children will also fill other bottles of the red, yellow, and green leaves. Teacher will fill these bottles with rubbing alcohol and hot glue the lids on. Children will make a guess if the colors will come out of these bottles. Check them each day. Did they both get the color out of the leaves? Which worked – water of rubbing alcohol? (the alcohol works) If they are interested, get a biology book and read together the reason one worked the other did not. If not, just enjoy the fun of getting the color out of the leaves. You can also try this with other things like vegetables.

Fun with Chemistry

You will need to have the follow items for this project:

small plastic spoon for each child	plastic magnifying glass for each group
craft stick for each child	package small bathroom sized cups
waxed paper	lemon juice
apple juice	water
tomato juice	vinegar
scissors	baking soda
a piece of paper and a pencil for each child	a small measuring cup for each group

Put a piece of wax paper on the table in front of each child. Give them a spoon and help them put about a ½ spoonful of the baking soda into their cup. Now ask the children to guess what might happen if they put some water in the cup. Next have them add a small amount of water from their measuring cup. Ask if it looked like they thought it would. Have them write a numeral 1 at the top of their paper and have them draw what the cup looked like after adding the water.

Now give each child another cup and put the baking soda in as before. Then give each group a small measuring cup with lemon juice in it. Then have them add a small amount of the lemon juice into their cup. Ask what happened? Did it surprise you? Have them use their stick to place some of the foam onto the wax paper in front of them and to examine it with the magnifying glass. Have them place a numeral 2 and draw a picture of what it will looked like after adding the lemon juice.

Continue on as before with the baking soda in their new cup and adding the other ingredients one at a time to their new cup. Have them examine each new combination and write the numerals with their drawings. Explain that when the baking soda is mixed with lemon juice it causes a chemical reaction. The lemon juice and the baking soda create a gas called carbon dioxide. The carbon dioxide is the fizzy bubbles in your cup. When you saw fizz in any of the other items added, it shows that there was some acid in it like in the lemon juice and it made a chain reaction too.

Fizzing Pictures

You will need unsweetened Kool Aid in several different colors, baking soda, saltshaker or other shaker bottles, vinegar, small sprayer bottles and white paper.

Have the children help you mix each package of Kool Aid with ¼ cup of baking soda. Pour mixture into shaker bottles. Children will sprinkle the mixture onto dry paper. Then have the children watch as you fill the small spray bottles with the vinegar. Turn the nasal on the spray bottle to produce a fine mist. Caution the children to only spray their picture and that vinegar can hurt their eyes. Supervise each child carefully while they spray their picture. Have them watch each others pictures as they fizz.

Remind the children that the baking soda and vinegar makes a chain reaction. The gas carbon dioxide was made from the mixture on their paper and that caused the fizz.

Fun with Rocks

Rocks can do many different things. Magnetic rocks can pick up things like paperclips. Sulfur rocks stink. Graphite rocks can write on paper. Pumice are stones that don't sink. They can float. You can purchase sets of rocks with special properties like these for $20 or less.

Salt and Pepper Dance

Items needed: balloons, wool cloth, plate with salt and pepper, string.

Blow up two balloons and tie them with the string. Place one of the balloons about an inch away from the plate with the salt and pepper. Observe that nothing happens.

Then set that balloon aside and rub the balloon well with the wool. Place the balloon about inch a far from the salt and pepper plate. Watch if for 3 or 5 minutes carefully or you won't see that the same grains of salt and pepper are attracted to the balloon, repelled, then attracted again over and over. They don't fall off, but are thrown by the electrostatic force.

Water Evaporation

Items needed: paper towels sections, plastic zip-lock bags, a fan and a blow dryer.

Children will wet four paper towels. Then they will put one the on counter and one in a zip lock bag. Then they will hold one in front of a fan. The last one will be placed on the table and the children will take turns holding the blow dryer over it. They will check to see what is happening with each of the towels during the day. At the end of the day, ask the children what happened to the water in the wet towels. Where did it go? Why is the towel in the zip-lock bag still damp? Talk about how evaporation from the air made the towels dry. Ask which towel tried the fastest? Why do they think it dried faster? Which one is still drying? Why do you think it is still moist?

GROSS MOTOR SKILLS

Washing Machine

Ask children how a washing machine works. Get them thinking about the movements of the clothes in it. Then tell them that they are going to pretend to be in a washing machine. They will move their bodies like the clothes in the washing machine. Use the CD *Jim Gill Sings The Sneezing Song and Other Contagious Turns* song number 4, "I Took A Bath in a Washing Machine." They love doing the actions again and again. This CD has many other fun action songs on it.

Circle Fun

Prepare slips of paper with picture actions and words with different actions on them. You can use stick figures for the actions pictures. Ideas to use are turning, jumping, hopping: feet together and on one foot, clapping, running, walking, touching toes, doing jumping jacks and etc. Put the slips in a small basket. Teacher will selected a CD with a strong steady beat for the children to listen. Teacher will also provide a stuffed bear to be passed around.

Have the children sit on the floor in a circle. Tell them that we are going to play a fun game. Tell them that they will be passing a bear around the circle to the music. Have them practice passing the bear around to the music making sure that they pass it in the same direction. Now tell the children that whoever has the bear when the music stops will draw a slip from the basket. Then we will all do the action on the card.

Try it out and correct any information that they might not have understood. Continue the game by playing the music again and stopping the song letting the person holding the bear draw a slip.

All the children will again do the action on the card. Be sure and take the slip used out of the basket that has been used. Play continues until the slips are gone. If time permits put all the slips back into the basket and resume the game until everyone has had a turn.

You control the music, so make it stop when the children who have not had a turn get a turn. If time is up, tell the children that you are writing down their names and that you will make sure they get a turn later. Then make sure you do it!

FIELD TRIP IDEAS

Call your local college or university science department. Ask if they would be willing to have students come to their classroom or lab to see some simple experiments preformed for them by students or professors. If not, try calling your local high school science department for help with this project. They might have seniors in a chemistry class that would be helping to show them some of the interesting things that they can do. Be sure and let them know that you will be having parents accompany your class to help with the children. Another place to try that involve science would be a bakery. Children could learn about yeast and how bread rises.

Music

GROUP ACTIVITIES/CIRCLE TIME

MUSIC AND MOVEMENT

Wee Sing Around The World by Pamela Conn Beal and Susan Hagen Nipp with Nancy Spence Klein, Published by Price Stern Sloan, INC, A member of The Putnam & Grosset Group 1994. This book includes the sheet music, words and a tape with singing by people native to each country and the authentic instruments. The songs are short simple young children songs from many nations.

Wee Sing Nursery Rhymes and Lullabies by Pamela Conn Beal and Susan Hagen Nipp Published by Price Stern Sloan, INC, A member of The Putnam & Grosset Group 2002. This book includes the sheet music, words and a tape with singing of each song. This makes it easy for you and the children to learn these sweet songs.

Heritage Songster by Leon and Lynn Dalllin, WCB, Wm. C. Brown Company Publishers. 332 folk and familiar songs with words, music, legends, cord symbols, guitar, ukulele, banjo, autoharp and piano included in it.

Diez Deditos Ten Little Fingers & Other Play Rhymes and Action Songs from Latin America, Selected, Arranged and Translated by Jose-Luis Orozco, Puffin Books Published by the Penguin Group 1997. The companion CD and others by him may be ordered by visiting www.joseluisorozco.com.

Teaching Peace Songbook & Teacher's Guide by Kathy and Red Grammer, Copyright 1993 Smilin' Atcha Music, Inc. This book also includes a CD of the songs for easier learning. These songs teach through song that we are all special and that we can live in peace with one another.

Music & Movement in the Classroom by Steven Traugh, CTP Creative Teaching Press, Inc. This and the tapes feature the Music of Youngheart Records' Greg Scelsa and Steve Millang. Designed for PreK-K.

Walter The Waltzing Worm Music book by Hap Palmer, Hap-Pal Music Inc. This book includes sheet music with words to songs and action directions, vocabulary, setting, variation and follow-up for each song. Tape includes all songs.

<u>Hap Palmer's Sally the Swing Snake</u> Music book by Hap Palmer, Hap-Pal Music Inc. This book includes sheet music with words to songs and action directions, vocabulary, materials and follow-up for each song. Tape includes all songs.

The five following CD recordings and one book by Jim Gill's are sold at www.jimgill.com

"Jim Gill's Irrational Anthem and More Salutes To Nonsense"

"Jim Gill Sings Do Re Mi On His Toe Leg Knee"

"Jim Gill Makes It Noisy In Boise, Idaho"

"Jim Gill Sings The Sneezing Song and Other Contagious Tunes"

"Jim Gill Sings Moving Rhymes for Modern Times"

<u>May There Always Be Sunshine</u> by Jim Gill. Jim's book and his CD's promote creative and active play. The songs are simple and young children enjoy them.

"Beethoven's Wig 4" Produced by Michael Geiger & Richard Perlmutter, Mangement:Regina Kelland for Beethoven's Wig, Inc. www.beethovenswig.com. Dance Along Symphonies.

To learn more about the following four CD recordings contact: 1-800-789-9990 or www. learningstationmusic.com.

"Children Love To Sing and Dance With The Learning Station"

"The Learning Station Here We Go Loopty Lou"

"The Learning Station Tony Chestnut"

"The Learning Station & Dr. Becky Bailey Brain Boogie Boosters"

The CD recordings include lyrics, actions and in the last one brain boosters. Children and adults enjoy the fun action dances.

"Kindness Counts" Music by Mr. Al and Lyrics by Dr. Becky Bailey www.mralmusic.com, www.ConsciousDiscipline.com.

"10 Carrot Diamond" by Charlotte Diamond. Fun songs that can be acted out.

"Kids In Motion" by Greg & Steve Youngheart Music. Songs for creative Movement. CD includes lyrics and tells the action to do while listening to it.

"Kiss Your Brain! Dr. Jean" Music arranged and performed by Mark J. Dye.

"Ole! Ole! Ole! Dr. Jean en Español!" Music arranged and performed by Mark J. Dye.

"Just For Fun! Dr. Jean" Music by Mark J. Dye.

"Over In The Meadow Dr. Jean Sings Silly Songs" Mark J. Dye.

"Dr. Jean & Friends" by Jean Feldman.

All of these songs are fun for children to sing while teaching children about singing and movement to music.

LANGUAGE AND LITERACY

Let's Get The Rhythm adapted by Anne Miranda, Scholastic, 1994. This book is a fun chant with good pictures to show the actions to do while using it.

Skip To My Lou adapted and Illustrated by Nadine Bernard Westcott, Trumpet Book. This book includes the sheet music for this song.

The Wheels On The Bus adapted by Maryann Kovalski, Scholastic. This book also includes the sheet music to this song.

Going To The Zoo by Tom Paxton, Scholastic, 1996. This book includes the sheet music for the song.

Walt Disney's Peter And The Wolf adapted by Walt Disney, Random House.

BINGO by Rosemary Wells, Scholastic INC.

Spider On The Floor Illustrated by True Kelly, Crown Publishers, a Random House company. This book also includes the sheet music for this song.

Play Rhymes collected and illustrated by Marc Brown, Scholastic. This book contains picture illustrating on how to do the many songs included in the book and the sheet music for six of the songs. The pictures are helpful for holding children's attention.

Five Little Ducks by Ian Beck, Trumpet Books, 1992.

Jiggle Wiggle Prance by Sally Noll, Scholastic.

The Eensy-Weensy Spider adapted by Mary Ann Hoberman, Scholastic. This book includes the sheet music and pictures with description of how to do the fingers actions.

The Bremen Town Musicians by Hans Wilhelm, Scholastic. The author grew up in Bremen, Germany and includes a note from the author.

Music Is In The Air by Ann Morris with photographs by Ken Heyman, Scholastic. This book has good illustrations of people performing and enjoying music.

Who Took The Cookies From The Cookie Jar? by Bonnie Lass & Philemon Sturges, Scholastic, 2000. This book has good pictures to help make it fun when you introduce this fun chant with clapping.

I Know An Old Lady Who Swallowed A Pie by Alison Jackson, Scholastic, 1997. This is a fun story to read after learning I Know An Old Lady That Swallowed A Fly. Children can also learn to sing it to the same music.

Eric Carle From Head To Toe by Eric Carle, Scholastic, 1997. This is a fun movement book with good illustrations.

Clickety Clack by Rob and Amy Spence, Scholastic, 1999. Use this book with the song "Little Red Caboose." They make a fun combination.

Cowboy Bunnies by Christine Loomis, Scholastic, 1999. I have used this book when I introduced western music.

Row Row Row Your Boat as told and illustrated by Iza Trapani, Scholastic, 2000. This book has great pictures to use before teaching this song. The sheet music is included in this book.

Teddy Bears' Picnic Illustrated by Bruce Whatley, Song arranged and preformed by Jerry Garcia & David Grisman, Harper Collins Publishers, 1996. This book includes a tape.

Fiddle-I-Fee adapted and illustrated by Melissa Sweet, Trumpet Book Published by Scholastic, 1992. This book has special pictures to help the children learn the simple song. The sheet music is included.

Scheherryzade and the Arabian Nights story by Constance Allen, text by Lisa Alexander, A Sesame Street/Golden Press Book. The book also has a tape to go with it. This book relates well the classical music of the Arabian Nights. Most libraries have the music on CD.

Froggy Plays in the Band by Jonathan London, Scholastic, 2003. A cute book that relates children to instruments.

Big Bird Meets The Orchestra by Liza Alexander. This book introduces instruments that are used in the orchestra. It has a tape to go with it.

Miss Mary Mack adapted by Mary Ann Hoberman, Scholastic, 1999. This book includes the sheet music and pictures with words showing the actions that go with the song. The actions are done with a partner.

Shoo Fly! As told and illustrated by Iza Trapani, Scholastic, 2001. Sheet music and a tape are also included in this book.

Song and Dance Man by Karen Ackerman, Scholastic. This book was given a Caldecott Medal. A great book to interest children in dancing.

Bam Bam Bam by Eve Merrian, Scholastic, 1996. This is a chanting book that boys will relate to.

The Lady with the Alligator Purse adapted and illustrated by Nadine Bernard Westcott, A Trumpet Book a division of Scholastic.

Do Your Ears Hang Low? and Other Silly Songs Illustrated by Pamela Cote, Scholastic,1995. This book includes the words with interesting pictures for many songs. There is also a tape.

Zin! Zin! Zin! a Violin by Lloyd Moss, Scholastic, 1996. This is a Caldecott Honor Book. There is also a tape for it.

Engine, Engine, Number Nine by Stephanie Calmenson, Scholastic, 1998. This book illustrates the popular chant with all the verses. There is also a tape.

Circle Time Sing-Along & Fingerplays by Susan Finkel and Karen Seberg. Contains song and finger plays, instructions, props/visual aids and extends.

Eye Winker Tom Tinker Chin Chopper Fifty Musical Fingerplays by Tom Glazer, Doubleday & Company, Inc., Garden City, New York.

My Toes Are Starting To Wiggle! and Other Easy Songs for Circle Time by "Miss Jackie" Silberg. 108 songs with circle time activities that develop motor, listening, language, cognitive, creative and self-esteem skills.

The Nutcracker: A Christmas Pop-up by Landoll, Inc. This book is great to read to the children before hearing parts music from "The Nutcracker."

SMALL GROUP ACTIVITIES/TABLE TIMES

MATH & COGNITIVE

Number Trail

Prepare a game board by using a half of a poster board for the base. Then add a trail around the board for the children to move their marker. Markers can be colored buttons or they can be other small objects. Place lines across the trails every 1½ to 2 inches. Now add cowboy stamps on some of the trail or draw small pictures. Write the word free under the stamps or the small pictures. Make dots representing number one through six on other parts of the trail. Put the word start at one end of the trail and finish on the other end of the trail. See example.

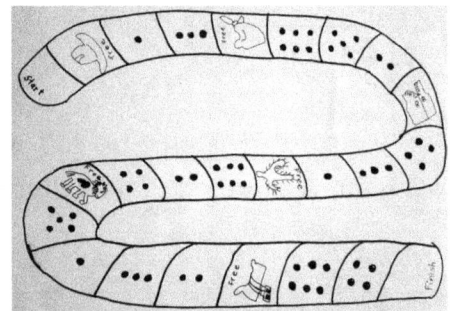

The children will use one die. They will take turns shaking a die and moving that amount. Then they will correctly identify the number that they landed on. If they name it correctly they can stay there until their next turn. If they did not name it correctly, they must go to where they were before. Landing on a picture is a free space and they can stay there until their next turn. They must all get to the finish line for the game to be over. When one or more children get to the finish line, they will become the cheer-leaders for the rest of the team.

If this is too simple for your age group change it by making the trail longer and using numerals on the board for one through six and number dots for seven through twelve. They will use 2 dice to play the game and they will play it the same way as the first game.

Wild West Memory Cards

Teacher will use plain, small index cards to make this card game. Write numerals 1-10 or if you want to make it more of a challenge use 1-20 on cards (one of the numerals on each card). Then on the other cards make dots for the numbers 1-10 or 1-20. Dots to equal one number per card. Then on the blank side use a sticker or stamp to decorate backs. They should all look alike. You can buy rubber stamps with western things on them.

To play the game place the cards on a table in rows with the numeral and dot side down. Children will take turns turning over three cards to see it they can make a match. A match is having the numeral match the correct number of dots. If they make a match, they can go one more time, but that is all. Then they must wait for their turn again. If they did not make a match, they turn the cards back over and place them back where they were.

Remind the children to watch where the cards were, so that they can make a match later. The next child turns three cards over and proceeds as before. Play continues until all of the cards have been matched up. It is a good idea to start with only a few of the cards so they won't be discouraged. Then when they get the hang of it add more cards.

Learn About Musical Instruments

Bring into the classroom different instruments each with a different kind of sound. For example a ringing instrument, a clicking instrument, a swishing instrument, a scraping instrument, a jingling instrument, and a drum would give the variety needed to show the kinds of sounds that may be produced. Let the children carefully select and try out an instrument and discover its special sound. Tell them that the instruments are not toys and that they need to take good care of them.

Next tell the children that you want them to explore an instrument and find out how many different sounds it can make. Now let them demonstrate to you how to play it and the different tones that it can make. Ask them if it can be played fast or if it needs time to ring. Also have them to play it louder or softer.

Then choose an appropriate song and have several children take turns playing their instruments with the song. You may also want to include a child playing a drum or other percussion instrument using a steady beat with the other instruments. Learning to make music together can be very rewarding for the children in social, cognitive and creativity development.

Match the Instruments

Obtain pictures of musical instruments from magazines, software, clip art or online. Copy the instrument so you have two copies of each and glue them onto small index cards. Now laminate them for durability.

Have the cards laid out on the table in front of the children with the instrument side up. Tell the children to take turns finding two instruments that are the same. When they have a match, tell them the name of the instrument and have them repeat it. Then the next child takes a turn. Play continues until all of the cards are in pairs.

This game will help them learn what different instruments look like and their names.

You can also use these same cards to talk about the different types of instruments and then have the children use the cards to group them into families.

Five Little Hot Dogs

Use this rhyme to help children count backwards from five to zero, recognize numerals or just for fun when they need to get their wiggles out.

> Five little hot dogs
> frying in a pan.
> The grease got hot
> and one went bam!

> Four little hot dogs
> frying in a pan.
> The grease got hot
> and one went bam!

Three little hot dogs
frying in a pan.
The grease got hot
and one went bam!

Two little hot dogs
frying in a pan.
The grease got hot
and one went bam!

One little hot dog
frying in a pan.
The grease got hot
and one went bam!

No little hot dogs
frying in a pan.
The pan got hot
and the pan went bam!

You can make the hot dogs and pan by looking at the example below. Attach the hot dogs to the pan by using Velcro. Write a numeral on each of the hot dogs (1-5). As you sing the song have children put paper hot dogs onto a paper frying pan. Have the children clap their hands together when the hot dog goes bam!

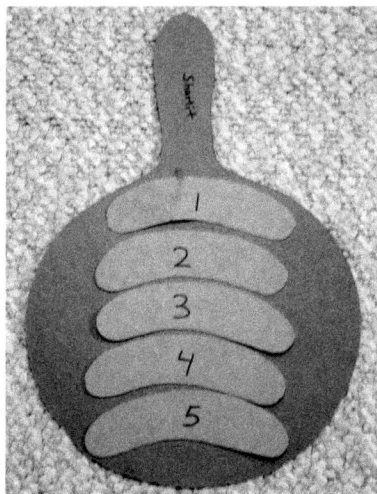

You can also sing the song by having the children hold up one hand and us their fingers for the hot dogs and their over hand as the pan. They will put the amount of fingers on the other (pan hand) to represent the number of hot dogs. Move the hot dog fingers back and forth across the pan as if was cooking, but when it goes bam, clap your hands together while saying bam. When the pan explodes, clap and say bam. This is a lot of fun for the kids as they learn to count backwards.

FINE MOTOR SKILLS

Cowboy Hats

Teacher will make a large cowboy hat pattern on poster paper. The children will use the pattern to trace around and cut out the hat. Then teacher can decide or have the children decide between these options. They could water color the hat. Stamp with rubber stamps and an ink pad. You could make their own simple stamps using sponges and mount them on spools, small blocks or wood or attach them with clothes pins. Then place poster paint on small foam plates for the stamp pad. Hat pattern shown below.

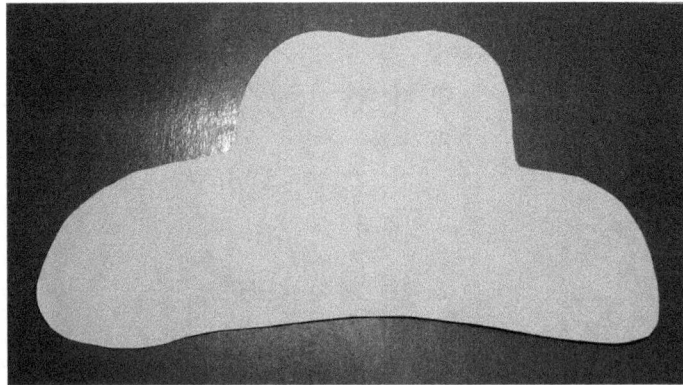

Guitar

Teacher will make a guitar pattern on poster paper for the children to trace and cut out. See example.

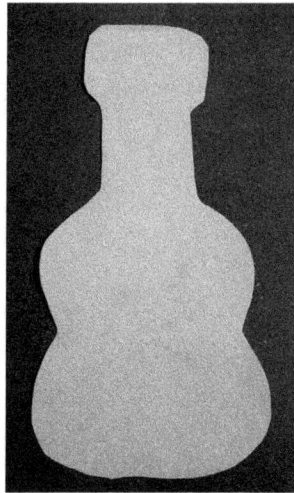

Use small bottles of school glue and place poster paint or food coloring into several bottles using different colors. The children will make lines and designs using the colored glue on their guitar to decorate it.

Sheriff Badge

Make pattern for the badge on poster board for the children to trace around and cut out. They can do his on colored paper or white paper. Next, the children will use a small bottle of glue to make designs. Or just have them use the glue to trace around the edges of the badge and trace the first letter of their name in the center of it.

Now provide a box lid or a plastic tray to place the badge in with the glue side up. Then give the child a bottle of glitter to sprinkle on the glue. They will tip the badge carefully sideways to release the extra glitter into the box lid. The extra glitter can be poured back into the bottle. When the badge is dry attach a safety pin through it and attach to their clothes or use a piece of masking tape made into a circle loop to attach it. See pattern.

Boot Pattern

Make a cowboy boot pattern on poster board for the children to use. They will trace around the pattern on colored construction paper and then cut it out. Supply colored noodles, beans or other collage materials for the children to glue on to it. See example.

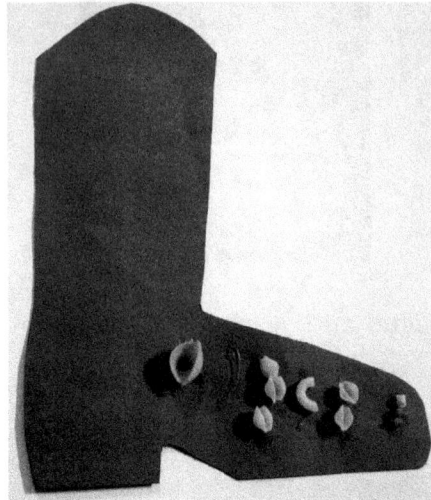

Neckerchiefs

Buy white cotton material for this project and cut it into triangles to form the neckerchiefs. Use cookie cutters with poster paint pads to decorate neckerchiefs. When they are dry, tie them around the each child's neck. See example.

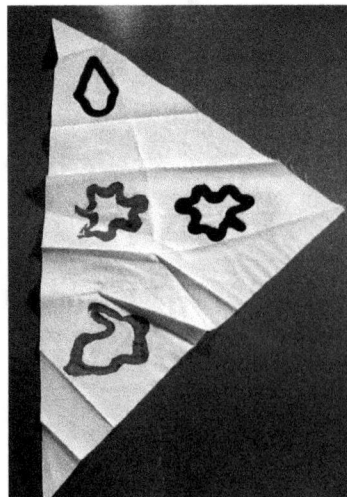

Paint With Music

Tell the children that you are going to put on different types of music and you want them to paint together a large sheet of butcher paper to the different types of music you will play. After each type has been played, remove the paper to dry and place new paper down. This activity can be during one day or you can have them do one different type of music each day. A good variety of music could include peaceful soft music, lively fast loud music, classical music with a full orchestra, music from different cultures and other music that is unique. After the papers have dried hang them up around the room.

Quilt Designs

The teacher will use gift wrap paper and or wall paper for this project. Use paper from a surplus outlet you can obtain inexpensively or buy end roll of wall paper from a wall paper store. Then use a paper cutter to cut it up into equal small one inch size pieces.

Show the children a real quilt or if you can't get one to show, find a good picture of one at the library and show it instead.

Let the children choose a colored piece of construction paper for the background. Then tell them tell them to take the square pieces of paper and make a design they would like for their quilt by laying in out on the background sheet. When they have it designed, have them lift up one piece at a time and glue it down. Continue one piece at a time until all of their pieces have been glued. See example.

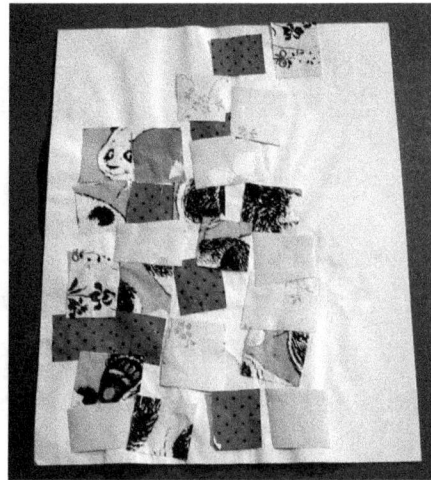

LANGUAGE AND LITERACY

Arabian Nights Activity

After reading <u>Scheherryzade and the Abrabian Nights</u> with the children use this small group activity. Copy some of the figures from your book to use only for your class educational purposes. Mount them on craft sticks for the children to use.

Tell the story in a simple manner using the characters on the sticks. Have the children listen carefully. Then take turns having the children retell parts of the story using the character sticks. This activity will help the children increase in visual and auditory memory skills.

Cowboy Book

After listening to different types of western music and reading books about early life in the West we will make a class book. The front and back cover for the book will be a horse head. You can choose a different shape for the cover of anything you would like. An example of my book's head is below. Next make pages for the book using the same shape to fit into the book upon completion.

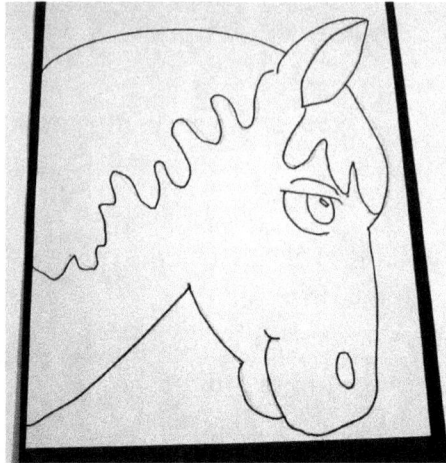

Have the children draw something that they learned about western life or something they would like to share about cowboys. They can use crayons, markers or colored pencils for this. When their drawing has been completed have them tell you about their drawing. Carefully write their words on a sticky note and place it on their picture with their name. Ask them if it's okay to write their words on their picture and if not write them on a separate piece of shaped paper next to their picture. Continue with each child at your small table before calling more children to the table.

You may want to continue this activity over the week so you are free to do other things with the children. You can also have a parent help you record the story of children as long as you train them how to do it before time.

Now read through the story and place the pages in the best order between the covers and connect together by punching two holes on neck side and put yarn or rings through holes to bind them together.

Read the book to the children and be sure and mention each person's name as you read their page. Then place the book in your library for the children to read. It will be a popular book for them. They will have increased their confidence in writing a story and their ability to read. They will want to read their page lots of time and will soon have the words memorized.

Where Is The Cowhand?

Buy plastic cowhand figures at a toy store or a Dollar Store for this activity. You will need a cowhand and a horse for each person in your small group to use.

Children will practice prepositions and matching skill. They will follow your directions, take turns and use listening skills.

Examples – Show and say: Put your cowhand <u>in</u> your hand and now take it <u>out</u> of your hand.

They will follow your directions. Put your cowhand <u>on</u> the horse, now <u>off</u> the horse. Put your cowhand <u>behind</u> your horse, now <u>in front</u> of your horse. Put your cowhand <u>over</u> your horse, now <u>under</u> your horse.

When they can follow your directions and say the directional word with you, have them take turns telling and showing other children the different directional words.

Sorting Game

Cut out pictures of four different categories from magazines. One might be baby items such as clothes, rattle, shoes, blanket, or a highchair. Another one could be different foods such as hamburgers, oranges, eggs, bread, carrots, and potatoes. Then do two more groups. After finding the pictures, place in sheet protectors, laminate them or put clear contact paper over them to protect them and so they can be cleaned.

Now have the children talk about each item in one of the categories such as the baby items and help them see how they all go together. Next do another category in the same manner. Then mix the two categories up and have the children take turns saying what the items is and which category it belongs. Continue until each of the picture items have been placed in the correct category.

Another day, introduce a new category and then add it to the other two categories already talked about. Then mix up all three categories and have them sort them. If they get one wrong, ask them what the picture of the item is and how it is used to help them understand the connection. Then when you feel they are ready introduce the fourth category. This activity is an ongoing activity, not to be done in only one week. Children will benefit in many ways from this activity such as vocabulary, classification skills and discrimination between like and different.

Music Listening and Expression

Bring different types of music into classroom on a CD/MP3. Pick short parts for the children to listen to before class. Then introduce the music and have them listen to it.

After listening to it, have them talk about how the music made them feel and use watercolor to express the movement in the song. Then play another piece and have them talk about the difference between and music. They may want to do another picture too. Continue on by dancing to the next piece of music instead of drawing to it, but keep talking about their feelings after each piece.

Cowhand Story

Make up your own story short story and make sure that you put three facts in the story that you want the children be able to recall. This is for the children to learn to listen for content.

An example follows:

Tom was a cowboy and he lived on a farm with his mom and dad. One day he asked his mom if she would fix him a lunch to take on a picnic. She put two sandwiches, a bottle of water and a dish for his dog in the bag, because he was taking his dog Fred with him.

Questions:

Who fixed Tom a lunch?

How many sandwiches did she put in the lunch?

What was the dog's name?

Do this activity with one child at a time, so you can see how many of the children need help. If a lot of children need to learn and practice this skill, use short information with the children daily and question them on the material covered. Keep track of the children's progress, so that you can help the ones that need it individually.

Learn About Instruments

Use the book <u>Walt Disney's Peter And The Wolf</u> with the CD music of Peter and the Wolf to point out various instrument that represent the charters in the book. Your local library will usually have this music with accompanying narration of the instruments.

Show pictures of the instruments used for the characters and have them listen carefully for them. Stop CD after listening and ask students which character they just heard. Have them listen for it again. If possible, obtain the sounds of each character and play them several times. Also ask them to see how the music sounds like the character.

This activity should be used at the end of the year when children are a little older and helps them develop discrimination of sounds needed for understanding words and letter sounds necessary for reading with meaning.

Xylophone

Cut out four different rectangles (in inches) 7 x 2, 5 ½ x 2, 4 x 2, and 3 x 2. Each rectangle should be in a different color. I used yellow, red, blue and green. Next center them on a piece of paper and connect them with wide line. Photo copy this sheet enough times so that each child will have one plus an extra one for your file.

Remove the construction paper from the copied page. Children will use the copied sheet to place the strips of paper you made onto them according to your directions. Tell them to find the tallest one and match to the paper. Then tell them to find the smallest one and place it on the smallest place. Now have them look at the two remaining ones and tell you which is the biggest and the smallest. Now have them place them where they think that they go. Check their work.

Next have them take all the pieces off the paper. Have one child at a time start from either end and tell you its size while placing the matching size on it. For example, they will say the bigger one or the smaller one. Then have them put the next size on it and label it next bigger or smaller until all of them have been labeled. When each child has done this have them glue the pieces onto their page and take them home. Tell parents to have children tell them the different sizes. See example.

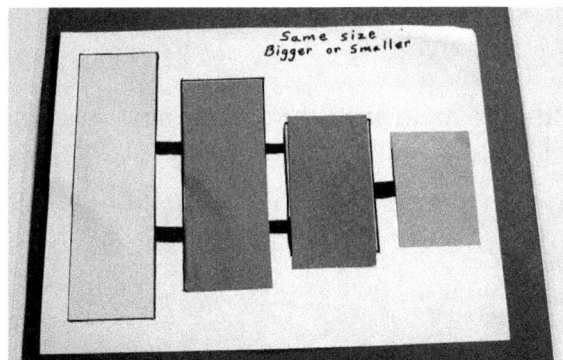

Cowhand Pocket Game

Teacher will cut a pocket off an old pair of jeans for this game. Cut slips of different colors of construction paper and obtain colored buttons to match color slips. The colors in this game should represent the colors children in your classroom need to learn or review. The game is played in the following manner. See example.

Teacher chooses one child to play the role of a cowhand and has the cowhand leave the group. Then the teacher will hold up one of the colored slips for the other children to see. Then the teacher will lead the group in singing the song.

This song is to the tune of "Where Is Thumkin?"

Cowhand, Cowhand,

We need you. We need you.

Please find a (say the name of the <u>color</u> shown) button.

Please find a (say the name of the <u>color</u> shown) button.

We thank you. We thank you.

The cowhand will put his/her hand into the pocket and find that color of button and show it to the group. Play continues by choosing a new cowhand and proceeding as before. When all the have been used you can start again or conclude for the day. If you have chosen to end for day proceed to having the children count with you the number of pockets each child has on them. Then ask children to tell you what they carry in their pockets.

FREE TIME

CREATIVE ARTS

Finger Paint

Make finger paints using the following recipe:

½ cup liquid starch

2 Tablespoons powder tempera paint

Mix the liquid starch into small bowl that has the powdered tempera in it and stir well. Place this mixture into a small container with a lid such as a small yogurt container. Then make several other containers using different colors of tempera colors. It is fun to use the primary colors of red, yellow, blue because they can make to many colors on their sheets.

You can buy regular finger paint paper or buy freezer wrap and use the shinny side to paint on. You can also use a different tray for each child to finger paint on. When they are ready to save their picture simply place a large piece of water color paper on top of it and have them help you smooth it over their paint. Now lift off the paper and you have a copy of their picture. They can then wash the tray off at the sink, so it will be ready to use again.

Shiny Paint

You will need a can of sweetened condensed milk and food coloring. Pour the can into several small paper cups (bathroom sized) then add a small amount of coloring to a cup and mix. If it is to light add more food coloring. Do the same thing with each of the other cups.

Children will use water color brush with water color paper to paint their paper. When it dries it will be shiny.

SENSORY

It would be fun to put sand into your sensory table or tub with small cowboy figures with horses and other props. You could add craft sticks for fences and tents with the addition of small size pieces of cloth. You could also add small rocks to make fire pits. The children could also add things that they make for the sensory tub. Let them be creative and enjoy the experience.

Another idea is to put Legos in the tub and see what they make in a different area than they are use to building. Let them add other props to it if they get you okay first.

DRAMATIC PLAY & SOCIAL DEVELOPMENT

Use different culture types of musical instrument, such as maracas, tambourines, drums, various stick instruments, bells, flutes and ukuleles. You can make some simple instruments to represent some of them. Oatmeal boxes can become drums with a little help from the children decorating them. Shakers like maracas can be made from empty contains like empty Pringle cans with rice or beans placed into containers. Tambourine type instruments from flying saucer toys with jingle bells attached around the edges using wire through holes you make.

The culture clothing to go with the instruments is important too. You may be able to pick some up at a thrift store. Scarves may be worn around the neck, over the head, over their face or around the waist. Any type of hat would also work. Large towels can become clothing when draped around someone or small ones can be draped around their head. Colorful material can be wrapped around their waist and tied or drape some over their shoulder and fasten on their using a belt at their waist. Full skirts that are the right length can be made smaller for their waist by sewing elastic to the inside of the waist band and pulling the elastic while sewing the elastic. Use your imagination and you will come up with even more ideas for clothing.

Keep a small compact CD player in the area too with music from different culture music to play on it. You can find these to check out in most library media departments. Tell the children ahead of time that the volume must be kept where you set it, so that it isn't too loud. Have lots of fun exploring different types of music.

SCIENCE

It is exciting to have children help you make music using glasses with water to tap with a spoon to create music. First put several empty glasses on the counter and have children tap them to see if they sound the same. Then put various amounts of water in each glass and have them listen to see if the sound is the same in each glass. Now have them experiment to see if they can make the sound higher or lower. Put the glasses on various surfaces to see if it changes the sound. Use soft things under glass and rubber under the glass. Help them discover that the vibrations make the sounds a little different.

You can color the water in the glasses, but help them see that the coloring does not change the sound. They may want to try putting other liquids in the glasses to see the differences too. Use thick and thinner liquids. Have them predict (guess) whether the sounds will be the same with thicker liquids. Tell them that are scientists now, because they are doing experiments.

GROSS MOTOR SKILLS

Obtain a square dance recording without the words of the caller or use the recording from MacMillan Sing & Learn Program titled "Color Hoedown." Tell the children that they will be learning a western dance. Do not use the music until they have learned how to do the dance slowly without the music. Then tell them that you will show them how to do each step in the dance. Do the dance for them from the instructions below.

First have them try side stepping in a circle to the right. Have them clap 1,2,3. Have them circle right again and have them go forward 1,2,3 and then go backwards 1,2,3. Now they will circle around again. Then they will stop and tap their foot 1,2,3 and circle around again. Now stop and take a bow.

When they can do it without the music well, add the music with you being the caller.

Say, "hold hands and step sideways to the right and go around the circle."

Then tell the children to "stop and clap their hands with a 1,2,3."

Them have them "circle around to the right."

Now call out, "walk forward 1,2,3."

"Then say "go backwards with a 1,2,3."

Now "circle right again."

Next say "stop and tap your foot 1,2,3."

Now "circle right again" then stop and "take a bow."

If have the recording just follow the caller in the recording. Have fun!

Another fun activity to do outdoors involves making a path out of cones that the children can follow. Provide stick horses for the children to use. Have them take turns follow the path marked with cones or arrows while galloping. If you do not have stick horses, use small children's brooms or thick dowel sticks with a poster board horse head taped onto it. It would be fun to also have them wear cowboy hats while riding their horse.

Mickey Exercise

Children will enjoy exercising with these cute Mickey Mouse ears you make for them. The example below is simple to make and the headband can be stapled to fit them. The recording is titled "Walt Disney Productions Mousercise" Song 1. Mousercise Medley – Mickey Mouse. The song really gets them moving.

FIELD TRIP IDEAS

Farm Visit

If you have any farms close by, call and ask if it would be possible to come to see what a farm is like and what they do there. Arrange for parent's permission and help with the children on the trip. Plan also to take a thank you card made by the children with you. Ask if they have a place where they could sit and have a snack while there. Be sure and talk to the children about how to act while there and to be careful with things. Make sure you clean up any areas you may have used on the field trip before you leave.

High School Music Department

Another interesting thing to do is ask a local high school music department if you could come on a field trip to see and hear the different instruments they play there. Ask if they could also touch or play a few of them like the drums or keyboard instruments. If they let you come, make sure the children know what to do while there, like listen and not talk while the teacher there is talking and to sit quietly when appropriate. Tell them that it is a privilege to go and see the instruments and to respect the instruments and people there. Also, arrange for parent's permission and help on the trip. Have the children draw pictures for them to say thank you and put them in a cover to take with you to give them.

Our Five Senses

MUSIC AND MOVEMENT

"The Cool Bear Hunt" from Dr. Jean Sings Silly Songs CD. This song evolves The five senses in a fun way. Children love to do this song again and again.

"Bubblegum" from Dr. Jean Sings Silly Songs CD. This song also is one that children love to do again and again.

"Five Senses" from Kiss Your Brain! by Dr. Jean CD, drjean.org.

"Five Little Monkeys" from Ole! Ole! Ole! by Dr. Jean en Español CD. This CD features songs in English and Spanish. Many children know this song and the movements already, so it's fun and easier for them to learn it in Spanish. The sense of hearing gets a good workout too.

"Special Me" from Ole! Ole! Ole! by Dr. Jean en Español CD. This song is a short song that you will want to sing weekly to remind the children that they are special.

"Wash Your Hands" from Touched by a Song by Miss Jackie CD. www.jackiesilberg.com. This song teaches children how and why to wash their hands.

"Who" from Kindness Counts Music by Mr. Al Lyrics www.mralmusic.com by Dr. Becky Bailey www.ConsciousDiscipline.com. This is a movement song that teaches about manners and kindness.

"Stick To The Glue" from Jim Gill Makes It Noisy In Boise, Idaho. www.jimgill.com This song has children pretended to have their hands stuck to lots of funny things.

"Poison Ivy" from Jim Gill Sings The Sneezing Song and Other Contagious Tunes by Jim Gill. www.jimgill.com. This song illustrated the sense of touch.

"Peanut Butter" from Barney's Favorites Vol.1. This song moves through children pretending to make peanut butter and jelly. Then to making a sandwich and getting it. Lots of fun for children and the music keeps them active.

"Apples and Bananas" from Barney's Favorites Vol. 1. This song will have children listening carefully to hear the change a letter makes to a new word sound.

"Spider On The Floor" from Singable Songs for the Very Young part 1 by Raffi. This song is fun and gets them thinking about how a spider would feel.

"Witches' Brew" from Witches' Brew by Hap Palmer & Martha Cheney. This song invites smelling, seeing and imaging how it might taste. It's fun to stir and add ingredients with the song.

You can use any songs this week that are fun for the children and help them enjoy learning, because they will all involve one or more of their senses.

LANGUAGE AND LITERACY

You Hear With Your Ears by Melvin and Gilda Berger, Scholastic Inc.

You Smell With Your Nose by Melvin and Gilda Berger, Scholastic Inc.

You See With Your Eyes by Melvin and Gilda Berger, Scholastic Inc.

You Touch With Your Fingers by Melvin and Gilda Berger, Scholastic Inc.

You Taste With Your Tongue by Melvin and Gilda Berger, Scholastic Inc.

Your Five Senses by Melvin and Gilda Berger, Scholastic Inc.

Sense Suspense A Guessing Game For The Five Senses by Bruce McMillan, Scholastic Inc.

Who's Making That Noise? by Philip Hawthorn and Jenny Tyler Illustrated by Stephen Cartwright.

Who Uses This? by Margaret Miller, Scholastic Inc.

Simple Signs by Cindy Wheeler, Scholastic Inc.

Say It, Sign It by Elaine Epstein Scholastic Inc.

The Noisy Book by Margaret Wise Brown, Scholastic Inc.

There Were Ten In The Bed Illustrated by Karen Young, Scholastic Inc. This is a book where children see animals from Australia in bed instead of common animals or children.

The Tale of Peter Rabbit by Beatrix Potter, Big Golden Book Golden Press. This book is a classic and it still has an appealing story for children. They can relate to it and it teaches values.

Seven Blind Mice by Ed Young, Scholastic Inc. A 1993 Caldecott Honor Award

Book. This is a great book that shows that we all need each other to understand and really see things.

Spider On The Floor illustrated by True Kelly, Song by Raffi Crown Publishers, Inc. This book shows the adventures of a curious spider.

The Napping House by Audrey Wood, Illustrated by Don Wood, A Trumpet Book by Scholastic Inc. This book is a wonderful picture book with delightful words.

When selecting books to go with the theme of five senses, focus on one sense at a time. Read it and ask children questions about the material. Then enhance the experience with activities. Then later in the day be sure to read a different type of book. The book should be an interesting story that uses their sense of seeing and hearing such as The Tale of Peter Rabbit.

Smell

Read a book on the smell sense. Then use some already prepared small clean empty margarine tubs. Cut a small circle hole in the tops of these containers, so children can smell the contents, but not big enough for them to see what it in them. Place a pieces of various items in each one. Examples of what to put in them are lemon, onion, orange, chocolate, tuna fish and vanilla on cotton ball. Put numbers on top of each container.

Tell the children that they are going to use their sense of smell today. Children will try to figure out without looking inside containers, what is inside each container. Pass them one at a time and have them raise their hand to guess after smelling the container what is inside. After several have made guesses open the container to see what was inside. Proceed to the next container as before. Continue until you have used all the containers. Now have them vote on their favorite two smells. Use a wipe off board to record the scents they liked and mark the number for each scent that you showed. What them help you tally up the number for each scent so that they can find the two most popular. A tie is okay too.

Touch

Another day read a book on the sense of touch. Prepare ahead of time one bag for each of the items you want them to touch and guess. Use simple things for them to touch and guess. Examples of items are a small, soft and fluffy teddy bear, a hard wood block, a piece of sand paper, a comb, a small hair brush and a smooth rock and so on, so that they all have an item to touch and guess.

Children will take turns placing their into the bag without looking inside and touching their item. Ask them to describe how the item feels like soft, hard etc. Then they will guess what the item is that they have touched. Have then have them pull it out to see if they were right. This continues while they are all interested. Stop before they have finished if they loss interest and are not listening to the other children and tell them that the rest to the children will have a turn later. Then after they have changed activities and got their wiggles out, let the other children have their turns.

Hear

Read a small book on hearing and then introduce the items you have prepared to help them learn to use their hearing to identify sounds. Before circle time use a tape recorder and a blank tape to record different familiar sounds around the house. Keep a record of the sounds and the order they were recorded. Some of the sounds I have used are: phone ringing, toilet flushing, blender that is blending, cat purring, dog barking, baby crying, hammer pounding, saw sawing, someone clapping, radio playing and some chopping.

Tell the children that you will play a tape of sounds and ask them to listen carefully listen to determine what is making the sound. Have them listen quietly until the sound ends. Then they may raise their hand and when called upon tell what they think has made the sound. Continue playing and discussing the sounds that they hear until all the recordings have been introduced.

See

Have this seeing activity made up before hand. Find large pictures of simple items like a dog or a car. Mount the large picture on heavy paper. Then plan where to place holes in a top paper that will cover the picture. The holes can be like doors with one side still connected on the side. In this manner it can be opened and closed. Place the holes so small parts of the picture can be seen when opened and glue or tape the top of the cover to the top of the picture page.

Children will take turns opening a window and making a guess by seeing what is in the hole. Continue until the picture as been identified or if no one can tell what the picture is, fold the cover back. Now have someone identify the picture. Discuss how they felt when they couldn't see the whole picture.

Taste

Read a book on tasting. Talk about the how the different parts of the tongues helps us to taste different types of things. Also talk about how our nose helps us to taste. Do an experiment by having a willing child be blindfolded. The child will taste a lemon while holding their nose so that they can't smell what the item is that they will taste. Have them lick a lemon. Then remove the lemon before opening their eyes and tell what they tasted. Then have them open their eyes and lick the lemon without holding their nose. Ask them if the lemon tasted sourer with their nose held or with it able to smell. Try this again using an onion. Discuss the differences it made in holding their noise.

Review

On the last day of the unit, review all the senses by using popcorn. Set up an air popcorn popper inside a box. Do not let the children see inside of the box. Tell the children to listen carefully to find out what is in the box. Also tell them to use their sense of smell to help them figure it out. Then plug in the popcorn popper. Soon the children will hear and smell it. They raise their hands and tell what they think it is in the box.

Tell them we will use our eyes to see if they and right. Show the popper and the popcorn. Ask what other sense they would like to use now that the can see, smell and hear it. If they don't get taste and touch help them figure that out with clues. Then put a little salt on it. Now have the children wash their hands and enjoy a small bowl full. Review what they learned while they eat.

SMALL GROUP ACTIVITIES/TABLE TIMES

MATH & COGNITIVE

Shape Outlines

Use a die cut machine to punch out shapes such as triangles, squares and rectangles or you can use shape punches found at craft stores. Also prepare large out lines of these shapes - triangle, square and rectangle. Children will choose a large shape and use the smaller shape pieces to fill in the large shape.

Have them try to put their pieces as close as they can to each other. Observe children as they do this and encourage them to turn small pieces in different angels to fill the shape. Use the shape name while children work with the shapes and encourage them to use the correct shape name also.

Fruit Loop Cereal Game

Provide each child with a small bag of cereal and ask them to sort their fruit loops by color. Then they will count each color group and with help write down the number of each color that they count. They will place each color in a line to count. Next they will place the next color beside the first color in a long line as they count and record the number in that group.

Children will continue in the same manner with the remaining colored cereal. Now they will determine by the number of each color and by seeing their lengths which is more than the other color. If lines of cereal look similar in length, they will use the number recorded to determine which is largest. They may also want to count them again, so that they can see that the length shows it is longer when using equal spacing between the pieces of cereal. Before working on this project have the children wash their hands and use the cereal on a clean space so they can eat the cereal after completion of the game or put them back in their bag for later.

Stamping Numbers

Prepare papers for stamping by folding copy paper sheets. Fold in half, then in half two more times to have 8 rectangles. If you want to have 16 squares fold in half one more time. Now write 8 or 16 different numbers in each rectangle or square. Next make a pads for stamping by folding a paper towel in half three times and placing each on a small plastic plate. Now mix poster paint with a little liquid dish soap and pour it onto the paper towel stamp pad. You can use different colors for each pad or the same color for all of them.

Having material prepared for this activity before time helps keep children on track. Hand out the prepared sheets, the stamp pads and new pencils with good erasers on them. Tell children to read each number in the square or rectangle on their papers and using the eraser part of the pencil press on paint stamp pad. Then stamp the dot shape in the rectangle or square by the number on their paper the same amount of times as the number written on it.

If they can't read their number tell them to ask you for help. Hold up the correct number of fingers for them to count that is written in their square or rectangle. Tell them to continue stamping until their paper has been completed. Keep a close eye on their progress to make sure that they are doing it correct and not just making dots. When their page is complete have them sit with you to go over their work to reinforce number names and counting skills.

Sparkle Bottles

You will need to collect clear clean water bottles for this activity. Be sure and ask parents for help supplying them. Also buy small colored rocks and glitter. You can find the rocks in the pet/fish department in stores such as WalMart.

Children will pick out and count from 1-10 small rocks or if you have enough and they can count to 20 have them pick 1-20 rocks. They will count their rocks with you and then they will each put their rocks into the empty water bottle. Now have them use a funnel to put a spoon full of glitter into their bottle. Now with the funnel in the bottle have them add water to their bottle using a small measuring cup. Fill close to top, about 1 inch from top.

Children will screw on the lid. Then they will use a permanent marker to write on their bottle the correct number of rocks in it. They will also write their name it. Now teacher will glue around the lid to keep it on. You can use a hot glue gun if you want it ready to shake or regular glue, but it will have to dry before shaking it. This is a good activity for the day you work on sight/seeing.

Sound Shakers

In advance, collect empty Pringle chip containers or other shaped contains that are clean and have lids. As in sparkle bottles, be sure and enlist parents to help you with the containers. Provide a bag of beans for the children to count and place into their containers. Have them put on the lids and shake them to see if it sounds just right to them. When it sounds like they want it, have them dump out the beans and count them for you. Now have them place the lid on and write the number of beans in their shaker as well as their name.

Later when all of them have completed their shakers have the children stand in a circle and pass out their shakers to them. Now play some music with a good steady beat and have the children shake them to the beat. Practice helping them shake to the beat. When they can do that, have them try to march and shake to the music. Try it later if they have a hard time doing two things at one time.

FINE MOTOR SKILLS

Pin Poke

Draw a variety of shapes such as a square, star, triangle, rectangle and a heart. This shapes will be placed on small squares of cardboard. Children will use pins to poke holes around the outline of the shapes that are on top of the cardboard. As they box on this project have the children tell you the shape that they are working. This work will help them develop their fine motor stills while helping them learn their shapes.

When the holes have been made around the outline, tape them on the window so that the light will show through the holes or place them over head on the ceiling light covers. Refer to the shapes often so that children learn all their shape names.

Listening Ears

Draw a pattern of a large ear on poster board and make several copies of it. Then cut around them. Use the paper cutter to cut construction paper in long strips of about 2 inches wide. You will need two of them for each child. Provide pencils ,scissors, construction paper and a stapler for children. Example shown.

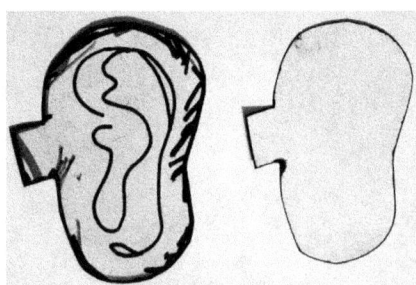

Now invite the children to the table and tell them that we will be making listening ears to use at circle this week. Show them the ear patterns and tell them that they will need to trace two ears for their head band. When they have traced them they will need to cut them out. Place the strips around their heard and then staple them to form a circle to fit around their head. Teacher will mark with an X where each ear should be staples. Children will then staple them with help from teacher. Make sure children write their names on their headband. Collect listening ears and pass them out at circle time to wear.

Match That Sound

You can prepare small containers such as empty film cartridges or small yogurt containers by placing different items in them. Some examples to put in them would be rice, marbles, paperclips, sand and liquids. Make matching containers of different types of items. Seal the lids by putting tape on them.

Then have the children take turns picking up one container and placing it in front of him/her. Then the child will pick up another container to see if he/she can make a match with the container in front of him/her. If it does not sound the same have the child move it away from him/her and pick another one to shake and try to match. Play continues until a match has been found. If the child is having a difficult time matching, have the other children help by saying it sounds the same or different when it is shaken.

Now the next child takes a turn finding a matching container for one that he/she chooses to shake. The child will listen carefully to find the container that sounds the same. Help the child if he/she has shaken all of them and has not heard the match in the same manner as stated before. Children will continue to take turns until all the containers have been matched up. Tell them that they have good listening ears to match all the sounds.

Nose Collage

Draw a large nose on poster board. Then make several copies and cut around them. These patterns will be used by the children to make a nose on construction paper. Provide different items for children to glue onto their nose picture. Some items that you could use for the collage are perfume pages from samples - cut small, scented strips, chocolate chips, Jello powder in different flavors, onion and /or garlic powder, cinnamon sticks, whole cloves, crushed basil and any other spices or herbs that have strong smell. See example.

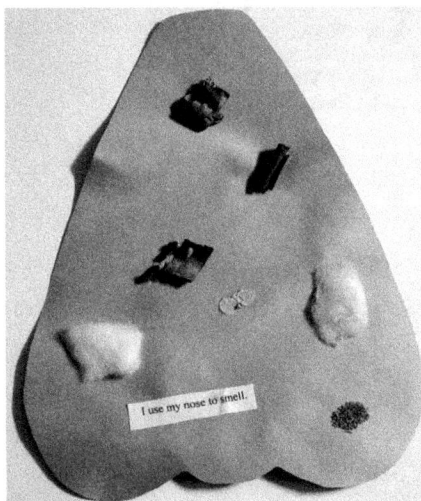

Children will select from the different scent items provided to glue onto their nose. They will arrange and glue them on their construction paper nose. Another item to have them glue on would be a slip of paper you have printed out on your computer saying, "I use my nose to smell." This will let the parents understand what they have been learning.

Feeling Hand

Draw a large hand on poster board. Then make several copies and cut around them. These patterns will be used by the children to make a hand on their construction paper. Have children trace the pattern of the hand, cut it out and glue items on it that have been prepared by the teacher. They might include: small squares of sandpaper, feathers, cotton balls, beans, small pieces of soft material, noodles, pieces of chenille, craft sticks, small foam shapes, elastic bands and paperclips. Prepare a slip to glue on the hand that says – I feel things with my hand. See example.

Finger Painting

Make instant pudding in several colors and flavors. Provide freezer paper or finger paint paper for children to paint on. Have the children wash their hands before doing this activity.

Children will receive two colors of pudding on their paper of their choosing without knowing the flavor of the pudding. Tell them to make designs on their paper with the pudding and have them taste it by licking a little off their fingers. Ask them to tell you what flavor they think each of the puddings are. Then tell them if they were correct and if not, to guess again. Before they are finished tell them the correct flavor and have them use their finger in the pudding to write their name.

Pizza

Purchase tube biscuits, pizza sauce and grated cheese at the store and have a small amount of flour available to keep dough from sticking to the counter. Also have a spoons for sauce spreading, tongs for placing the cheese on pizza, hot pads for holding the hot cookie sheet and a large cookie sheet to place the pizzas on to cook them. Line it with foil and put masking tape in squares across the foil with children's name on a square so that they will know where to place their pizza.

Tell the children that they are going to make their own pizza and that they need clean hands to keep germs from their food. Have them wash and dry their hands. Sanitize the area where they will be working. Open the tube biscuit container and give each child a biscuit. Show them out to lightly dust their hands with flour so the dough doesn't stick as easily. Then show them how to flatten the dough with their fingers and make a circle. Now have them spread the sauce on using their spoon and using the tongs to place cheese on their pizza. Now teacher will place their pizza on the sheet where the child points to their name on the foil for their pizza. Ask them if they can smell their pizza and what things they can taste.

When all the pizzas are on the tray and the oven has preheated to the temperature on the label, place tray in oven and set the timer. Watch it carefully so that pizza is light brown. Then take it out and cool slightly. Have children wash hands again and sit at clean table to eat their own pizza.

LANGUAGE AND LITERACY

Tricks and Tasting

Prepare small containers and label contents on the bottom.

1. One container of sugar and one of salt.

2. One of powdered sugar and one of flour.

3. One of sour cream and one of plain yogurt.

Show the two containers that look alike one group at a time. Ask the children if they think that they are the same thing. Have them vote yes they are the same or no they are different. Now give each child a tiny sample of each pair. Ask if they taste the same of different. Then ask them to describe how they taste, such as sweet, sour, salty or bitter. Then show them the label and tell them what it is that is in the containers.

Then do the second container set in the same manner as the first pair. Next do the third set of containers in the same manner again. Now ask them what they learned about seeing and tasting things that look alike.

Picture Categories

Use magazines to locate pictures to mount on paper and then laminate. Find pictures for items that your children will be familiar with, such as baby items, bathroom things, kitchen items, toys, and clothing. Spread out the pictures and ask students to find pictures of things that go together. Have them work together. Help by giving clues when needed, such as can you see things that a baby might use. After they have them sorted have children take turns telling about the items in one of the groups.

Now have them tell you the names of the items and why they go together. Continue with another child and a different group. Proceed in the same way until all of the groups of pictures have been talked about. If children see pictures that they think belong in a different group have them tell you why they belong in a different group. Be ready to be for surprises in their answers and respect their ideas.

Sound Bingo Game

To make this game, purchase a CD at a school supply store or make your own by taping sounds, writing what you have and then finding pictures to place on their own bingo cards. You could use the computer/internet to find the pictures you need. When the cards have been made, play the sound and then stop the recorder when children look on their cards for the picture that matches that sound. Sounds like a clock ticking, baby crying, car horn honking, T.V. playing, keyboard typing, water running, feet walking, someone laughing, washing machine running, toaster popping up, blender running and many other sounds help the children learn to listen closely and develop a better vocabulary.

Have them put smaller markers on each sound that they hear and when they have five in a row have them say bingo. Now have them name each item that they heard and check it with your list of sounds that you have played. Then if the player had correct sounds he/she is a winner. Give the child a sticker. The players will dump their markers off their card and teacher will continue the game by playing the sound tape. When they have heard all the sounds that you have you can stop the game or start tape and game over again.

Feeling Walk

Prepare ahead of time items for the children to walk through with their bare feet. Some of the items I have used for this experience are, quilt batting cut into a square, a pail of sand, bubble wrap in a large bubble size, crushed ice, heated rice bags, a pail of gravel, a large piece of foam, a pail of wild bird seed and a pail of warm water is last this towels waiting for them to dry their feet on. Then talk about how each of the items in the walk felt. Everyone has a turn and then we do the walk again one last time. The children love it and it helps the learn to express themselves. Ask several parents to help you with this activity so that shoes and socks get back on the correct person and feet get dried.

Whose Picture Do You Have?

The teacher will prepare this activity by taking pictures of everyone in the classroom. Then the teacher will have a few of the children sit in a small circle. Tell the children that you will be placing a picture of a child from the circle on a back of a child in the circle. The teacher will show the children in the circle the picture of the one of them before placing it on the person's back.

The child picked will start asking questions of the people in the circle. He/she will try and discover whose picture is on their back. They can not ask the name of the person on their back, but ask questions such as: Am I a boy? Do I have brown hair? Can I run fast? What color are my eyes? Do I have on blue? As the child listens to the answers to the question he/she must decide which child is most like the answers being given.

Then when she/he thinks they know who the child is that is pictured on their back says, I believe you are (name). If he is right that child gets to pick the next child to stand in the circle and she/he sits down in the circle. Now the teacher puts on new child's back the picture to guess and the game proceeds as before. This game ends for the day when the small circle children have all had a turn. Another day select another small circle then do the game as before. Continue this game on additional days until everyone has had a turn. Their vocabulary, reasoning and knowledge about others in their class will increase.

Children Voices

Use a tape/audio recorder with a built in microphone or regular one if you have one. Record each of the children, one child at a time. Do an interview with them telling you their full name, how old they are, what their favorite color it, their favorite foods are, their favorite game and or toy is and if they have brothers or sisters. Then each day during table time play one child's interview for they other children to hear. Tell the children ahead of time to try and remember something about that person. When the child's tape has played ask each child to tell one thing about the child that hasn't been mentioned by another child yet.

This is good practice for listening skills and it also helps the children learn about each other. This might be fun to do with the children at the first of the year and then later. You could play the earlier tape and then the later tape so that the children could see how much they have grown.

FREE TIME

CREATIVE ARTS

Provide shaving cream for the children to finger paint in on the table top. Let them have fun smelling and drawing with their fingers whatever they would like. Then when it is time to clean up, show them how to use a window squeegee to clean the table off quickly. Another child can wipe off the table after that and all children can help wipe off their aprons.

Sack Puppets

Use small lunch sacks for the puppets body. Then have different colors of construction paper for parts of the body, glue, markers and pencils to draw body parts and scissors to cut them out. You could also provide wiggle eyes, buttons, ribbon and material. Let them have fun creating their own person and maybe they will include senses like hands, eyes, nose, tongue and ears too.

Scented Pictures

Use scented markers for the children to draw whatever they would like. They enjoy smelling the markers as they draw.

Jello Painting

Prepare a small package of Jello as you normally do. Set the Jello in fridge until it starts to slightly thicken up. You can use different colors of Jello on the same day or wait until another day for more colors. Cut sponges into one inch pieces or wider for children to use. Teacher will place Jello in small bowls for the children to use. Then children will dip their sponge into the slightly thickened Jello and they press down on a piece of paper to create a design. Encourage them to press lightly to keep from making puddles on their paper. Ask them what it smells like.

SENSORY

Warm Water

Put warm water in the sensory table or tubs with different size bottles funnels and measuring cups. Add some dish soap while filling the tubs or table by running the water into the dish soap. Children will enjoy the bubbles, warm water and the pouring.

Pretend Baking

Put flour in the sensory table or bins along with sifters, measuring cups, mini cupcake pans, small size bread pans, small bowls, spoons for mixing, wire whips, and various molds for forming. Have the children wear aprons for this activity and limit the number of children that can be there at one time. Have a clipboard for children to sign their name on if they want a turn there. Have children cross off their name when they have a turn. They can also sign up to play there again, but they need to sign their name at the end of the list. Keep a close eye on the table and do not let children throw flour. If they spill it's okay, but have a small size broom and dust pan so that they can clean up after themselves. They really enjoy this activity and surprisingly they do a good job keeping the area swept up.

DRAMATIC PLAY & SOCIAL DEVELOPMENT

Children love to play doctor. Set up a doctor's office with a waiting area with magazines and chairs. Also a check in desk with telephone, writing paper, pens, pencils, envelopes and a cash register for payments with play money. Have available dolls in different sizes for the moms and dads (children) to use as their sick children.

Next area have a examining table for the dolls to lay. Have a good supply of ace wraps, toy doctor kits, empty pill bottles and a supply of real bandages for the doctor and nurses to use. You may have the children sign a paper on a clipboard to have children take a turn playing in the area. Have them cross their name off when they have a turn. Leave this area up all week or longer depending on the interest children show in it.

SCIENCE

Feeling Hands

Have the children help you make these items for the science table. Teacher will provide rubber gloves for this activity. Children will help for fill each glove with a different thing. Then you will tie the end closed. Some items you could use to fill gloves are rice, beans, cotton balls, flour, sand and small Styrofoam balls. The children enjoy helping fill them. A funnel is helpful for filling the gloves. Children enjoy feeling the gloves after they have been filled. They all feel so different. Ask them questions about how they feel.

Seeing Sense

Children will also help you make the "seeing sense items." You will need clear clean bottles with lids, food coloring, cooking oil and/or baby oil, glue to seal the lids and water. Put water in bottle until it is 2/3 full. Then add one of the oils and finally the food color. Now put the lid on tightly and seal with glue gun or regular glue. When the bottle has been sealed have children carefully shake the bottle to see what happens. The other bottles can be made in the same way, but using different colors, less or more water and oil. Just make sure the bottles are full and the cap is sealed on. Another variation you can do is to add small plastic items such as beads or small figures to the bottle. You can also add glitter. Have fun making many different bottles and shaking them so see what happens. Have the children try to figure out why the oil always goes back to the top of the bottle.

GROSS MOTOR SKILLS

Dancing with Music

A fun activity to do is play the song "On the Count of Five" from Sally The Swing Snake by Hap Palmer. This song have the children in a circle moving their hands, feet and other parts of their body. If you don't have this song have them do this song "The Hokey Pokey." You can find this song on children's recordings you can check out at the media center of your library. I found it at the library on the CD "All-Time Favorite Dances." This CD also has other fun dances like "The Bunny Hop and the "Mexican Hat Dance."

Another fun activity is to ask children how a washing machine works. Get them thinking about the movement of the clothes in it. Then tell them they are going to pretend to be in a washing machine and they will move like the clothes in the washer with their bodies. I use the CD "Jim Gill sings The Sneezing Song and Other Contagious Tunes" by Jim Gill song #4 "I Took A Bath in a Washing Machine." It has the children doing lots of fun movement.

Animal Walks

Have children walk like a cat or dog by crawling on hands and knees and meowing or barking. Then do a bunny by having them squat low on their heels, putting their hands flat on the floor

and jump forward. Another fun animal to do is a duck. This is done be bending knees and putting your hands around their ankles while walking forward one foot at a time, but remaining in the knee-bent position and quacking.

FIELD TRIP IDEAS

Take children for a short walk outside to a near by park or school play ground. While on the walk have children use their eyes for seeing birds, clouds, trees and flowers. Have them listen for different sounds and identify them. Have them feel tree trunks. Then have them create a picture of the bark by rubbing a crayon back and forth across tree truck. Also have them touch the soft grass with the bottom of their hand while moving it over the top of the grass. Plan for a snack to eat when you get to your destination. This could be cheese and an apple or anything simple. Be sure and take water and small cups to have with their snack. Take lots of pictures of the children and parents who go with you.

Here is a list of other important things to take and do on the trip. Have parents go with you. Take a camera for pictures. Take a small first aid kit including a telephone and a list of all the children and parent names with their phone numbers. A blanket to sit upon for the snack. Paper and crayons for the tree rubbing, sun screen if it's sunny or coats if it is cool. Also have each of the children go to the bathroom before you leave. Bathrooms are not always open at parks and play grounds. If possible have one adult meet you there.

Other places to go would be a children museum. They are wonderful places to go where children are free to explore by touching and feeling things and trying things out. They usually offer discounts for groups of children. If parents could pay for their own ticket it would help you out on the cost of the trip. Use the list from above for important things to take, but leave out the crayons and paper for the tree rubbing.

Where To Get What You Need

There are many different places to get what you need. If you use your imagination, many items can be substituted for what you have on hand, can get for free, etc. For example, you may have an abundance of baby food jars from a family toddler. You can easily convert these to be part of a project. Teaching is also about being resourceful. Have family, friends, students and yourself save:

- Baby food jars

- Toilet paper rolls

- Paper towel rolls

- Scraps of material

- Extra tile

- Extra pieces from home improvement projects

- Coffee cans

- Oatmeal containers

- 2 liter bottles

- Cereal boxes

- Egg carton

- Milk jugs

- Salt containers

- Anything you can think of to be re-purposed for a learning tool

Other places to get materials include:

- Home improvement stores (Lowes or Home Depot)

- Dollar Stores

- Educational Supply Stores

- Grocery Store

- Party Supply Store

- Online Resources:

  — Oriental Trading Company: www.orientaltrading.com

  — http://www.etacuisenaire.com

  — Many great songs and activities are available from http://www.newbridgeonline.com/, which is where you can find the MacMillan Sing and Learn songs and other activities. Use the search function and type in "songs for learning". You may also be able to find these used online at www.alibris.com, www.amazon.com, or www.abebooks.com.

www.ingramcontent.com/pod-product-compliance
Lightning Source LLC
LaVergne TN
LVHW081320060426
835509LV00015B/1599